COMMUNITY
CENTRE
DESIGN

Edited by Santiago Gonzáles García

© 2013 by Design Media Publishing Limited
This edition published in September 2013

Design Media Publishing Limited
20/F Manulife Tower
169 Electric Rd, North Point
Hong Kong
Tel: 00852-28672587
Fax: 00852-25050411
E-mail: suisusie@gmail.com
www.designmediahk.com

Editing: Santiago González García
Editorial Assistant: Janice Yang
Proofreading: ZHANG Chen
Design/Layout: YANG Chunling

ISBN 978-988-15664-4-7

Printed in China

COMMUNITY
CENTRE
DESIGN

Edited by Santiago Gonzáles García

Design Media Publishing Limited

INTRODUCTION

Community centres are public locations where members of a community tend to gather for group activities, social support, public information, and other purposes. They may sometimes be open for the whole community or for a specialised group within the greater Community. In this book, community centre guidelines have been prepared to support those involved in the planning, design and operation of community centres. The document contains information about what makes a successful community centre and outlines practical steps for consideration in planning and designing a community centre. They have been developed in consultation with local government partners and reflect the collective experience and expertise of those who have planned, designed and managed community centres for many years. At the same time, this book presents manynew selected community centre projects all around the world with numerous photos and drawings.

CONTENTS

Chapter Two – Design of Community Centre

PREFACE

In this book, there is a compilation of 25 examples of Community Centre, in which a wide range of architectural typologies is included, through which we can see the different ways to resolve the functional programmes that the buildings destined to the Community service require. The Community Centres are spaces of coexistence, knowledge, leisure, culture and education. Therefore, they are dynamic and living spaces that are designed from the perspective of a combined and non-discriminatory participation. The space favours the social bond that is established amongst the members of a community and, in many cases, improves social and cultural relations which hadn't existed before the construction of these centres. The elimination of the architectural barriers boosts the accessibility of all the people, independently of their physical capacities, what turns these community centres into integration centres which allow full participation of all people and facilitates the interaction and the diversity.

The projects collected in this book deal with sportive uses, swimming pools, auditoriums, children schools, meeting rooms, etc., that is to say, all the spaces that are required to be turned into meeting and activity points of the citizens. The characteristics of the physical surroundings and the demand of the community are the features that in occasions define the basic premises of the uses intended for the centre. The programmed uses in each population generate and stimulate activities that improve the quality of life of its members. Some of these uses take a specific importance contributing the main feature of the building around which other complementary uses are arranged.

All the buildings express, by means of their architectural style, their will to turn into referential iconic elements in their urban environment. The image and arranging of their external volumes that invite to organise the life of the neighbours around the spaces created both in their interior and in their outside: in their courtyards, squares and gardens. These centres, therefore, benefit the appearance of the urban surroundings where they are located when proposing spaces designed for a pleasant use that propose diverse architectural and constructive solutions, adapting to the programme of needs and to the physical space. Some of the shown projects expand and recover some existing buildings. These interventions provide new uses and renew their image in accordance with the new formal tendencies of architecture. This involves an achievement in updating some installations, by incorporating new technologies and new materials that offer improvements in the technical and structural quality, in the energetic efficiency or in the removal of architectural barriers. It promotes, in addition to an urban renovation, the possibility of transforming older buildings with a new own entity, by redesigning their previous architecture with contemporary elements.

In all these centres there is a special concern about the sustainability and the energetic efficiency. The buildings are meant to obtain the maximum use of the natural energies, such as, sun exposure conditions, ventilation or insulation… at the same time as they respect the nature consolidated in their surroundings. In some of them, some existing big trees are incorporated to the architecture, sometimes turning into natural protagonists of the building. This investment responds to the necessary tendency of the architecture to the natural resources in a rational way and minimise the impact in the environmental surroundings. These projects take into account the energetic systems that boost the saving, the materials of construction, the physical and natural surroundings where they are located, the recycling… In short, they contribute to the improvement of the quality of life of the members of a community.

The built surface, and therefore the scale in each one of them, is very variable, depending on the functional program that is resolved and of the population to which they give service, covering from small buildings for a neighbourhood to big complexes formed by several buildings like community centres of the city. In any case, independently of the scale, all these community centres put their architecture to the service of a common aim: the creation and design of spaces for meeting and coexistence where an important part of the social relations is developed. It is a design that meets diverse factors, but that transforms physically and socially its surroundings.

Santiago González García
Architect Director of NAOS ARCHITECTURE

reference & design guidelines

for community centre design

Yoga Room of Arlington Free Clinic, designed by Perkins + Will, photo© Kenneth Hayden Photography.

1. COMMUNITY CENTRE

1.1 Overview of Community Centre [1]
Community centres are public locations where members of a community tend to gather for group activities, social support, public information, and other purposes.

Community centres may sometimes be open for the whole community or for a specialized group within the greater community. Examples of community centres for specific groups include: Christian community centres, Islamic community centres, Jewish community centres, youth clubs etc. (http://en.wikipedia.org/wiki/Community_centre)

Parks are also considered community centres. Another pioneer of community centres was Mary Parker Follett, who saw community centres as playing a major part in her concept of community development and democracy seen through individuals organizing themselves into neighbourhood groups, and attending to people's needs, desires and aspirations. This can also include parks.

In the United Kingdom, the oldest community centre is possibly established in 1901 in Thringstone, Leicestershire by the old age pensions pioneer, Charles Booth (1847-1916). Extended in 1911 and taken over by the Leicestershire County Council in 1950, this centre still thrives as an educational, social and recreational community resource and was the inspiration for numerous others of its kind.

There are also community centres for a specific purpose, but serving the whole community, such as an arts centre.

Some community centres are squatted, sometimes rented buildings, mostly in Europe, which have been made into organizing centres for community activities, support networks, and institutional initiatives such as free kitchens, free shops, public computer labs, graffiti murals, free housing for activists and travelers, recreation, public meetings, legal collectives, and spaces for dances, performances and art exhibitions. Those in a more established setting may be directly connected with a library, swimming pool, gymnasium, or other public facility.

Community centres have various relationships toward the state and governmental institutions. Within the history of a given institution they may move from a quasi-legal or even illegal existence, to a more regularized situation.

In Italy, from the 1970s, large factories and even abandoned military barracks have been 'appropriated' for use as community centres, known as Centri Sociali, often translated as social centres. There are today dozens of these across Italy. The historic relationship between the Italian social centres and the Autonomia movement (specifically Lotta Continua) has been described briefly in Storming Heaven, Class Composition and Struggle in Italian Autonomous Marxism, by Steve Wright.

Social centres in Italy continue to be centres of political and social dissent. Notably the Tute Bianche and Ya Basta Association developed directly out of the social centre movement, and many social forums take place in social centres.

In the United Kingdom there is an active Social Centre Network, which aims to link up 'up the growing number of autonomous spaces to share resources, ideas and information'. This network draws a very clear distinction between the many autonomous social centres around the country and the state or large NGO sponsored community centres.

1.2 Role of Community Centre

Community centres play an important role in our communities. They provide places where people from a range of backgrounds and interests can interact, learn, recreate, be supported and grow. At the same time, in many areas, they are the focus of socially sustainable communities. It is important that we think creatively about these centres to ensure we develop innovative facilities that reflect our changing lifestyles and community needs. We

Huis Van Droo

need to explore new ideas and ways of delivering programmes, services and activities which are essential to our daily lives.

2. OVERALL PRINCIPLES FOR SUCCESSFUL COMMUNITY CENTRES [2]

Community centres range from small community halls and meeting rooms available for use by the community to large multipurpose centres that incorporate a wide range of services and facilities.

As these guidelines are intended to be applied in a wide variety of settings, the definition of community centres used here is a broad one, and refers to: publicly owned facilities that provide space for local organisations and community groups to meet, and for a range of social programmes, services and activities which address the social needs of a community.

A community centre may provide:
• General community use space for meetings, activities or events.

• A base for the delivery of local community services and programmes.
• Particular services, programmes and activities for specific target groups, such as young people or older people.
• Space for hire for private functions.
• Specialist facilities providing a particular focus on recreation, arts, cultural activity, learning or social support.
• A number of these functions within a single centre.

Despite the numerous models and diversity of uses, the essence of community centres is that they support the development of socially sustainable communities by providing physical spaces to help address the social needs of a community.

2.1 Address Community Needs and Promote Social Outcomes

• A community centre should address the social needs of the particular community in which it is located in order to contribute to residents' and workers' health, wellbeing and quality of life.
• Programmes, activities and services offered should respond to the needs and interests of the people that live and work around it.

Centennial Community Centre

• Programmes, services and activities should foster long term social benefits for the community.
• The planning and design of a community centre should reflect the potential programmes, activities and services envisaged.

2.2 Provide a Range of Community Services, Activities and Programmes
• Successful community centres should be well used, both day and night, throughout the week and weekend. This requires a range of activities that provide for the needs of a variety of user groups.
• Centres that are designed to be multi-purpose are generally better able to accommodate diverse groups and uses.
• A mix of uses helps to ensure that a centre is not la-belled as a particular 'type' of facility or available only for a particular target group, and that it is perceived as a facility available for the whole community.

2.3 Contribute to the Public Domain and Sense of Place
• Community centres can act as important focal points and gathering places and provide important public spaces for a community.

West Vancouver Community Centre

The Culture Yard

• Whether a large, iconic building, or a smaller, more intimate place, a strong connection between a community centre, its users and the broader community can mean that the building is seen as a reflection of local culture and an intrinsic part of that community.

2.4 Support Community Cohesion
• Community centres have the potential to bring a variety of people with different circumstances and backgrounds together to build community cohesion.
• Community centres should facilitate social interaction between different groups in a community and help to nurture and develop networks, linkages and cooperation.

2.5 Develop a Strong Local Profile
• Successful community centres are well known in the community and recognised widely as a source of information and support.
• A strong local profile is important to ensure that there is high community awareness of what the centre does.
• Services provided at community centres need to be promoted and marketed to the local community to ensure high levels of community usage.

2.6 Involve the Community
• Successful community centres involve the local community in planning, design and delivery.
• Providing opportunities for local people to be involved in the life of their community, and to develop and use civic skills, are important functions of community centres.
• There may also be opportunities for local people to participate in centre management, as well as planning activities and daily operation.

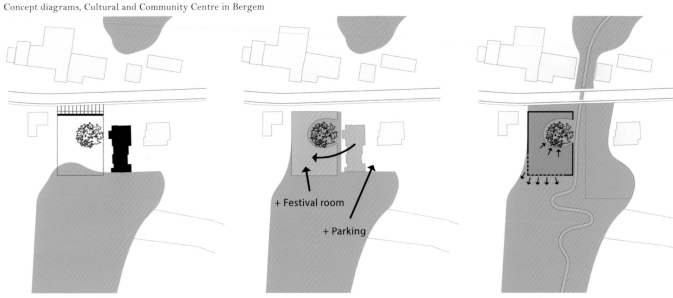

Starting Position:
- No connection between
  the green zones
- Dilapidated existing building
- Forgotten tree
- No festival room

Intermediate Phase:
- Existing building in use until
  new building is operable

Final State:
- Connected green zones
- Performed tree
- Festival room open
  to tree and landscape
- Parking as part of the park

2.7 Promote Physical Integration

• Successful community centres are positioned to integrate with other uses and services. Effective stabilization can be maximized by locating community centres with or near schools, shops, public transport or other community facilities such as libraries.

• By positioning a community centre within a hub of activity, the centre can help to create a true focal point for a community. Its useability is also improved when a range of services are situated together in a convenient location.

• Potential impacts such as noise and privacy need to be considered.

2.8 Provide a Diversity of Programmes, Services and Activities

So that community centres can serve the whole community, a diverse range of programmes, services and activities are required. These need to respond to the specific needs of the community and social outcomes identified.

Practical ways to encourage high levels of use and a variety of activities include:

Centennial Community Centre

• Fund staff to identify community needs and organise and deliver programmes, services and activities.
• Establish/support a local resident management group to activate the centre.
• Provide support and encouragement for voluntary resident involvement.
• Develop hiring and fee policies which promote equitable and affordable access for a variety of groups and ensure that the centre is not monopolised by single groups or interests.
• Provide seed funding for community initiatives that will support the development of programmes, services and activities.
• Identify outreach and sessional services which can be delivered at the centre.
• Have a local organisation or service agency located within the centre that can initiate activities and services.
• Prepare a services plan/business plan for the centre.
• Consider partnerships with other local services and community organisations for the development and delivery of services, activities and programmes.

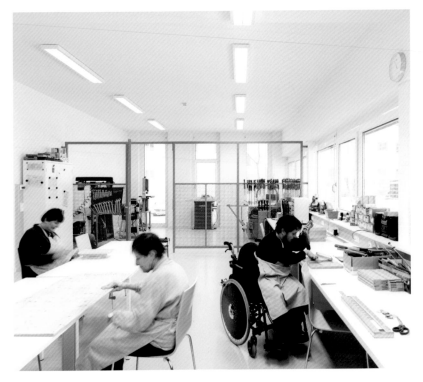
Lebenshilfe Weiz Centre

The Culture Yard

2.9 Encourage Staffing of Centres

Successful community centres often have regular staff to initiate and support activities. Staff can also be important in ensuring there is a good mix of activities and the centre is not monopolised by particular interest groups. They are also often critical in developing and supporting services and programmes for high need target groups to enhance the social benefi t of the centre. Staffing of community centres has been an ongoing difficulty, given the very limited availability of government funding for community development.

While capital funds are available through developer contributions, recurrent funds for staff have not been available through this mechanism. As a result facilities may be built, but not effectively operated.

Options for staffing of community centres include:
• Secure recurrent funding for community development workers for a specified period through planning agreements negotiated with developers/ delivery partners.

The Culture Yard

• Encourage the local council to employ staff to manage/program centre operations. Particularly in larger council-owned centres that provide multiple functions and user-pays activities, councils may provide staff to run activities and manage the centre.
• Accommodate a local funded community organisation with a broad community development focus in the centre.
• Apply for funding for a range of projects which may support community programmes operating from the centre.
• Design the centre to provide office accommodation for local services. In return, service staff can take on centre management and programming roles and/or use centre meeting/activity rooms for services and programmes.
• Incorporate income generating activities with income used to employ staff. Income generators may include fee-paying courses, business sponsorship, and rental from leasing space to businesses/government (such as cafes, complementary professional office and/or government departments).

Whatever the size, location, model or management of a community centre, the objectives and principles outlined in these guidelines should be

The Culture Yard

addressed. These provide guidance on the 'big picture' issues that need to be considered in planning and delivering successful community centres. Successful community centres result from the right combination of a number of inter-woven factors that reflect the needs and circumstances of their local community.

Community Centre, Gersonsvej

Batesford Reserve Community Centre

The Community Centre Guidelines present overall principles and key factors for planning, designing and operating community centres. They have been developed through consultation with local government partners and reflect the collective experience and expertise of those who have planned, designed and managed community centres for many years. These guidelines encourage and support those involved in the planning, design and operation of community centres. It is anticipated that these guidelines will assist in delivering high quality outcomes for all stakeholders and successful community centres which are used and enjoyed.

3. COMMUNITY CENTRE DESIGN GUIDELINE [3]

While planning issues such as size, scale and location are critical to creating successful community centres, how centres are designed and delivered is equally important. When planning for new or growing communities, we have a unique opportunity to maximize the potential social benefit ts of a community centre by ensuring its design:

Community Centre Senhora da Boa Nova

• Enables the centre to respond to community needs.
• Strengthens its presence in the community.
• Is functional and practical.
• Promotes the efficient use of resources and effective delivery of services.

3.1 Identify Local Social Needs and Desired Social Outcomes
Community centres should be tailored to the social needs of the community they will serve. Replicating a standard model from elsewhere is unlikely to adequately meet the particular needs of the local area.

Key tasks include:
• Determine the age, lifestyle, cultural and socioeconomic characteristics of different groups within the population and their likely interests, expectations and preferences with regard to community activities, programmes and services.
• Consider the needs of workers and visitors to the area.
• Determine priority needs and the social outcomes and benefits that the center will aim to achieve.

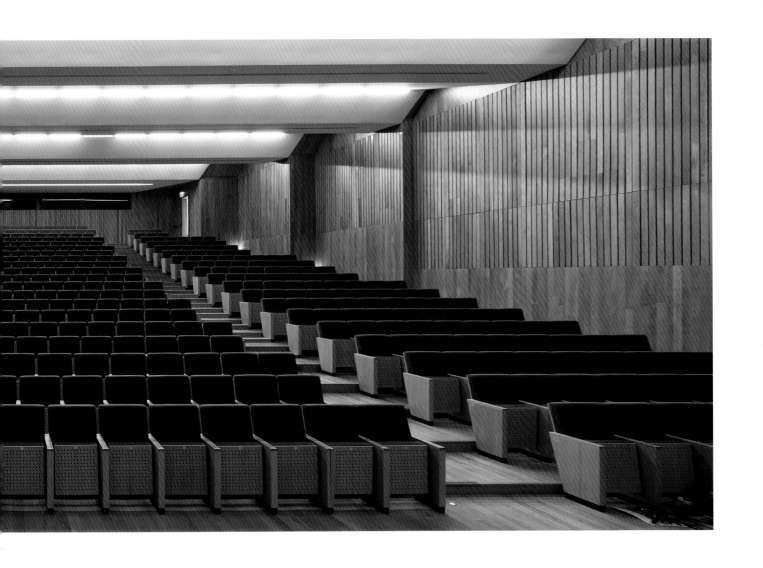

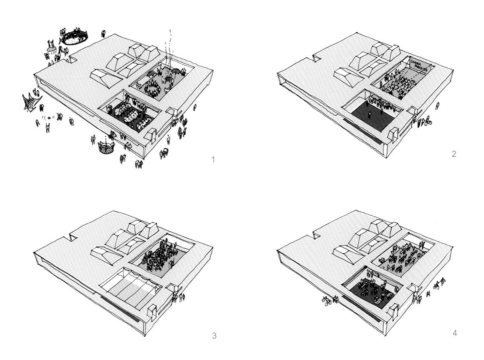

1. Festival, 2. Cinema, 3. Church service, 4. Car boot sale, Community Centre, Zeilsheim

Community Centre Senhora da Boa Nova

• Identify whether the need is for a centre with a broad generalist or specialist focus, for instance a particular focus on recreation and young people, or cultural activity, or providing services for disadvantaged groups.
• Consider the availability of other community facilities in the district. It may be appropriate to expand or upgrade an existing facility nearby, rather than build a new one.

3.2 Determine Size and Scale

When it comes to community centres, one size does not fit all. There is no minimum or standard sized catchment population that triggers a requirement for a community centre and no ideal scale or size for a facility.

Community centres are provided for catchment populations of varying sizes, ranging from as small as 3-4,000 people in some areas, up to district or sub-regional level facilities for populations of 40-50,000. They may comprise a simple hall or a large complex with multiple staff andextensive programmes.

Site plan, Community Centre, Gersonsvej

Centennial Community Centre

Centre of Social Services in Montealto

3.3 Identify Location

To be well utilized and serve identified social needs, community centres need to be accessible and visible. Community centres should be located so that they:

• Are central to their catchment area and provide equitable access to all potential users. It is important to remember that the catchment area does not necessarily correspond with development area/local government boundaries.

• Are accessible by public transport (i.e. Public transport stops within 400 metres walking distance).

• Have good pedestrian and cycling connections.

• Are on a main street with ground floor street frontage for optimum visibility and accessibility.

• Are clustered with other facilities, such as shops, schools and public libraries to promote convenient access and help create a focal point for community activity.

• Are not sited to conflict with neigh bouring uses.

• Have room to expand and adapt as needs change.

• Are near open space, to allow for related outdoor activities and community events, such as festivals and markets, where possible and appropriate.

• Are near sporting, recreation and leisure facilities, to create a health and activity focus, where possible and appropriate.

3.4 Consider the Functional and Design Features

Community centres should:

• Be appealing, attractive and quality buildings, that contribute to civic pride and the character and identity of a place.

• Consider symbolism that communicates history, community values and future aspirations, expressed through public art and architectural elements.

Ibaiondo Civic Centre

• Be easily identified and known by the community as a public facility for community use.
• Enable passers-by to see what happens inside the centre and what it is used for.
• Provide a range of spaces suitable for a variety of activities and user groups.
• Provide multi-purpose spaces capable of being configured into different sizes and for different activities.
• Allow for concurrent activities by different user groups.
• Be designed so that different functional areas can enhance social interaction, but also minimize potential conflict associated with privacy and noise impacts.
• Provide a safe and secure environment, especially for night users (incorporating crime prevention through environmental design principles).
• Be designed to be flexible and adaptable to meet changing user requirements.
• Include spaces designed to reflect the desired uses of the centre. These might include, for example, kitchens capable of use for private functions, facilities to support creative activities or performing arts or office space for service providers.
• Be designed for the life cycle groups likely to use the centre now and/or in the future and provide facilities appropriate to their different kinds of needs (for example, nappy change areas, children's play areas, 'youth friendly' spaces, or features for older people with limited mobility).
• Have the ability to lock down different components to provide managed access at nights or on weekends.
• Have the potential for separate entry/exit points for particular facilities, such as youth activities room.
• Provide direct access from activity rooms to adjoining outdoor areas for

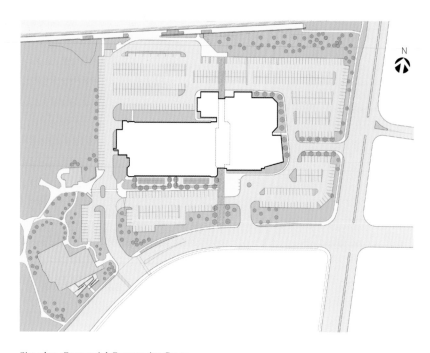

Site plan, Centennial Community Centre

children's play and social events.
• Incorporate energy and water efficient design principles and promote sustainable use of materials including waste minimization.
• Include adequate space for storage that allows for different user groups' equipment to be secured when not in use.
• Have adequate parking, including parking for a community bus and bicycles, within safe walking distance and which is well lit at night.
• Have high quality broadband access.
• Provide safe drop off/pick up areas and pedestrian access for centre users.

3.5 Co-locate with Other Facilities Where Appropriate
Co-location involves shared or joint use of facilities and often the integrated delivery of some services.
Opportunities and advantages of co-locating community centres with related facilities such as schools, libraries, recreation centres, child care facilities and community health centres need to be considered in the planning and design of community centres.
Co-location enables:

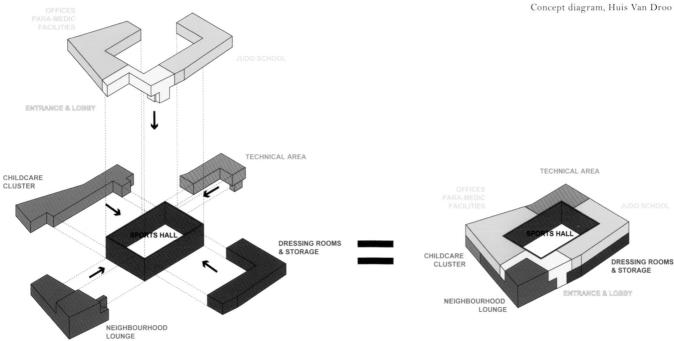

• Pooling of resources to provide better facilities.

• The concentration of compatible services and facilities to create a community focal point.

• Improved access and safety for users who can access a range of services at a single location.

• More integrated and innovative delivery of services.

• More efficient use of land, for instance through shared, rather than separate, parking areas.

3.6 Develop Sustainable Management, Maintenance and Policy Arrangements

Many community centres are run by community based volunteer management committees, while others are managed directly by councils or by the local organisations which occupy them as part of a tenancy arrangement.

In developing sustainable management and maintenance arrangements for community centres, a number of models may be adopted.

Killarney Ice Rink Community Centre   Killarney Ice Rink Community Centre

Issues to consider include:

• Ensure management arrangements are adequately resourced with appropriately skilled people capable of managing the centre effectively for the long term.

• Consider the sources of income likely to be derived from centre activities that may be available for management and maintenance of the centre. These may include regular income from user fees, hire charges, rent from sub-tenants or commercial income generating activities, such as operating cafes or running monthly markets.

• Balance the need for recurrent funding streams with considerations of affordability and equitable access for all target groups.

• Ensure the centre can be kept clean and wellmaintained, as presentation and public image are critical for the centre to be well utilised. Employed staff and management committees should be welcoming and representative of the community in which the centre is located.

• Ensure centre hiring, allocation and events policies promote fair and equitable access and support the social benefits expected.

• Ensure social benefits of centres can be monitored and reported on by setting and measuring performance targets.

• Consider the strengths and weaknesses of establishing community management committees comprising volunteers from the local community. While this model promotes greater levels of community involvement and ownership of a centre and helps build community capacity, it may be difficult in some areas to attract and retain volunteers with the necessary skills and expertise to manage the centre.

• Consider the strengths and weaknesses of a Council employed manager. While this helps ensure effective day-to-day management and may be the only option in new areas where volunteers and community organisations are not present, it lacks some of the community involvement benefits of

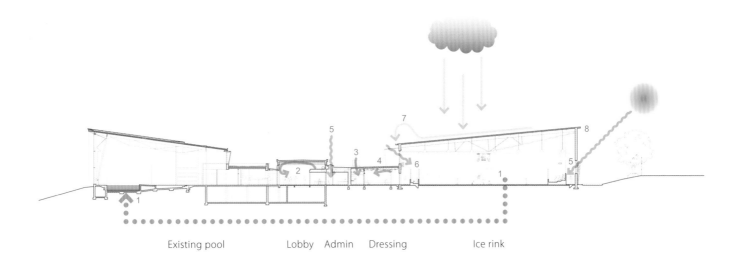

Existing pool   Lobby   Admin   Dressing   Ice rink

other models. It may also rely on the centre being operated as a major commercial enterprise, with the cost of management offset by user charges and commercial activities.

• Consider the strengths and weaknesses of management by a community organisation or service provider as a tenant of the centre. As discussed above, while this model can ensure a regular presence at the centre, potential disadvantages are that centres can become identifi ed with particular organisations and associated with their type of service, and may not appear accessible to the broader community.

Sustainability Diagram (Top):
1. Heat recovery coil - energy is captured and re-used to heat the pool
2. High efficiency mechanical unit for air handling
3. Economizers + variable air volume systems on air handling units
4. Demand controlled ventilation via CO_2 monitors
5. Natural daylight to interior spaces
6. Daylight control to reduce energy consumption
7. Rain flow control
8. High performance envelope

4. IMPROVEMENT AND PERFECTION OF CENTRE DESIGN [4]

Centres and environment have a unique architectural individuality and space sequence characteristics. Therefore, architects should create a high quality environment according to local geographical features, historical tradition, and the traits of residents' activities. Building image is an orderly perception as a whole, it is reflecting the building internal logic, strength, composition, aesthetic feeling, and characteristics. The architectural image of centre buildings is different from other recreational building types because of its function and the uniqueness of spatial constitution: pay more attention to the beauty of contour and the fluency of facade lines; the surface and body are simple; there is less block cross, change and combination pay more attention to architectural detail processing; the volume mainly be dignified and generous yet brisk and lively; lay more emphasise on cultural continuity and traditional inheritance of the centre itself. The centre building should be identifiable. Centre building always demonstrates its unique formal beauty because of its distinct characteristics.

The land on which the building is situated is composed of rock, corresponding to the hillside with a strong slope, and that it gives its name to the neighbourhood, Monte Alto (High Mount). It was necessary to find the dimension in which place the building. So it was very important to integrate an easy access from the street to the users, in addition to find the orientation towards the outside views.

It also had to find a way of linking the building to the rear of the building, in the slope that continues to rise.

It's for this reason that we decided to build a platform halfway up that sorts different areas of the building and their access.
(NAOS ARCHITECTURE, SOCIAL CENTRE IN MESOIRO)

Outdoor environment of a centre often includes a large area of green space, colourful waterscape and landscape features with different styles, which requires attentive work on both design and construction. But the shortage is the form of a facility is greater than its function, the visual effect greater than using effect; the amount of space for people to do various outdoor activities

Community Centre, Gersonsvej   Community Centre, Gersonsvej

is small, comfortable degree is not enough. For example,some centres have the problem of space quality itself: the venue is narrow, with poor ventilation, unreasonable equipment, etc.; some mixed cafe, reading space and a billiard room together in a large space which has no proper separation that makes a noisy atmosphere and play, rest and reading influence to each other. Thus it can be seen that deliberation on the quality of centre design is important. Such 'small' problem often fails to attract the attention of designers. As the more and more limited space in the modern city, the environments and the detailed design are closest to people, and any trace of visual pleasure will have a positive impact on people.

Today, the Boa Nova Community Centre includes Nursery, Day Centre for the elderly, social assistance services, a public canteen, and a public gymnasium. The building has 4,800 sqm and 5 floors (2 above entrance level and 3 below.)

At the design stage, we were dealing with a public building of a reasonably large scale; however, we wished the main façade to be welcoming and warm, providing the sense of entering a home,

Community Centre, Gersonsvej

Community Centre, Gersonsvej

rather than presenting the notion of entering a public building. The first design strategies were two: first, to place the building perpendicularly to the main entrance; and second, to locate the entrance on the fourth floor, taking advantage of the site's steep slope. With these design strategies, we managed to reduce the apparent scale of the building.

This community centre included many programmes and activities. The hardest design task we faced might have been bringing together spaces which responded efficiently and comfortably to functions with very diverse needs and scales. The community centre needed to provide, on one hand, small scale spaces suitable for private functions (such as the nursery's sleeping rooms, or the social assistance offices, etc) while, on the other hand, was required to host larger scale louder groups (such as the children's playrooms or meetings for small groups up to 50 people). We decided to place the spaces hosting larger groups closer to the ground floors, while keeping the nursery's private area on the upper floor. We further designed a large hall at the entrance which we used for organizing and dividing the circulation needs of the different groups.

Furthermore, the Community Centre needed to host community events which could easily reach a turnout of 1,000 people. For these large scale events, we decided that using of an outdoor

Ibaiondo Civic Centre

private space was the most efficient solution, considering the site's mild weather. Hence, we designed an outdoor courtyard accessed only from within the Boa Nova and protected, by the buildings, from the stronger winds. Thus far, this courtyard is the heart of the Boa Nova site, holding community events which have reached 3,000 people. On a daily basis, the courtyard is used both as children's playground and as a terrace overlooking the steep valley and the distant seashore views.

(Francisco Vaz Monteiro and Filipa Roseta, Community Centre Senhora da Boa Nova)

In general, it should meet these following principles and requirements during the centre design: clear partition, rational layout, easy to contact, not disturb each other; reasonable and efficient organisation of transport, necessary outdoor venues; the venue designs should be adapted to local conditions, compact, saving land; fully consider the site's objective natural conditions and cultural. landscape, in harmony with the surrounding environment, and coexist with the environment.

For us the main issue is always how the building interacts with the environment where it is situated. Thus for the community centre one of the biggest questions was how to make the intimate environment in the open field where the building was situated – the answer was creating additional inner courtyards, that form intimate outside area for the community functions.

In Sōmeru Community centre the government building is united with the local library, club and day centre for elderly people. Thus the house is meant to create a real meeting place for locals and also a place where they can meet and interact with the local government.

(Salto AB, Sōmeru Community Centre)

Social Centre in Mesoiro

4.1 Perfection of Functional Facilities

The spatial using features and functional requirements are decided by people's activity, so the centre has complexity in its architectural space, transport and daily life are mixed on the community street, private life and public space are blended, diverse functions coexist in the same space. Functional complexity means the diversity of connection between them, though not fully independent from each other. It shows space wide adaptability and maximize human behaviour activities in it.

Design a community centre for an architect is an exciting challenge project, it is necessary to solve a diverse program and in many cases heterogeneous and contradictory programme: reconciling fluently uses such as pool, theater-auditorium or library, allowing free flow of users simultaneously that control them with minimal control personnel, etc.

Undoubtedly, a civic centre among other activities offers social and administrative services to the citizen, decentralizing public services towards the different neighbourhoods of the city. A building of these characteristics generates significant operating and maintenance costs, so it is essential to pay attention to the economic criteria, attending from the number of workers needed for daily use, to the efficient control of their energy consumption.

From the first sketches made, our concern in this regard focused on designing a place friendly and provocative at the same time, a place of personal enrichment where citizens interact visual and spatially with groups of a diverse range of leisure, sport and culture activities. A place to enjoy, spaces that allow seeing and being seen. To project a building of this features is necessary to know in detail the characteristics and scope of the various activities that will be carried out inside. Secondly, it is highly recommended to study factors as diverse as the relationship between different uses, the location on the site, or adequacy of the overall design of the building (lighting, accessibility, spatial flexibility, etc.). It is necessary to promote

Temple Sinai Community Centre

flexibility and interaction between the different functions of the building. The major difficulty lies not so much in architectural design, but to enable efficient control of building users, or the integration of the different facilities, as well as maintenance derived from a demanding public use.
(ACXT Architects, Ibaiondo Civic Centre)

Designers should take different groups of residents into account, especially the functional needs of different age groups, different cultural background populations. Under the circumstances that residential area is large, the residential group which the centre serves are complex, it should pay more attention to analysis of the needs of different groups. As part of some countries are currently facing the aging of population, the elderly resettlement problem has gradually attracted the attention of the whole society.

On this occasion, in the centre to only provide activities suitable for young people and only notice fashion consumer demand is unreasonable, such centres are not able to become the centre of the entire residential

Can Ramis community centre and multipurpose building   Can Ramis community centre and multipurpose building

community. Elderly and children are vulnerable groups in transport, who have strong dependence on residential area, so the centre should have more activity space for them.

One of the difficulties of the buildings was the combination of two applications for very different age ranges. On the one hand, for children from 0 to 3 years old and on the other for people older than 70 years old with physical problems that needs special attention.

For children, the choice of materials is very influenced by their own safety.
- Continuous and soft floors to protect falls and because children are permanently playing on the ground, with nice colours and textures.
- Materials in the walls and floors easily washable and hygienic.
- Doors with security systems to prevent that they trapped fingers
- Different elements that incite to the game, to play and the curiosity, vivid colours and textures, mirrors.
- Toilets that are designed for an infant scale
In summary, the building is designed from a height of 60 centimeters use, to make the children feel the building provided to them.
For against, another area of the building for the elderly, is designed for people with very different needs of use and other conditions.
- Heavy-duty and hard floors to give them security in the tread.
- Handrails for support on the routes of hallways and rooms
- Bright spaces: a very open building towards the outside views to allow the contemplation of the landscape and even to view the activity of the playground.
- Walking areas in courtyards outside but controlled areas to avoid the lack of supervision of the elderly.

Applications in both cases are of course independent and do not mix at any time, but it has

Centre of Social Services in Montealto

managed to give and image of unique building as Public Centre of Social Services, with a reference as building architecture to the neighbourhood.
(NAOS Architecture, social centre in mesoiro)

Centre function is based on meeting the needs of different age groups. In addition to the setting subjects, emphasis on the importance of supporting design of the subjects is also necessary: such as the comfort degree of the floor, the height of the step, have wheelchair ramps or not, have children handrails or not, etc. Therefore, tea room for the elderly, children's game room, and fitness room for the young people, the difference lies not only in different equipments in the same space and different equipment requirements, as well as different ancillary detailed requirements.

The idea of the mixed functions that actually came from the client is very important. We tried to create a building that really invites people to enter it, a building that is transparent and welcoming but also cozy at the same time.

Huis Van Droo

Huis Van Droo

In Sōmeru each of the main function is arranged around one separate courtyard inside the building – one for entrance/government, one for hall/day centre and one for library. Thus everything is very closely connected but all the different functions can also work separately not disturbing each other.

For us the main principle for the materials was that it would have a friendly and lively impact. The façade made of wooden sticks attached to concrete panels provides a shimmering effect as one passes the building. The use of similar wooden material in interior provides a smooth interaction of inside and outside.

As the programme was quite small, we decided to make one-storey building so that all the building is on the same level and extremely easy to use also for elderly or disabled people. It should be visible that the building is really meant for the locals to use it. One has to design in the way they will feel there at home.
(Salto AB, Sōmeru Community Centre)

Designers should also take the different groups of users, even accompanied and viewer's needs into account. Such as children's playroom in the centre, if the designer did not notice the relationship of connecting activities, and did not set the rest seat for adults around children's playground, then parents can only be standing around the instrument, and also don't have a good communication atmosphere, the situation will be very embarrassing.

Designer can set tea room or café adjacent to playroom, or design a high steps bar space in the children's playroom, so adults can watch the children play without worries and can enjoy their own fun in a comfortable way: chatting, reading newspaper, playing chess. This harmonious atmosphere calls for designer to conduct a detailed study and do a careful design.

Cultural and Community Centre in Bergem

Laurimar Community Centre

4.2 Character and External Space of Building

Community centre design should be subordinated to the habitability requirements of the community. During the design process the first thing to deal with is the proportional relationship of the overall building, the proportional relationship between each volume and scale of the components, and do the best make it close to people, and create intimacy and a sense of belonging. In addition, the community centre is the social activities centre, it should have a significant and unique art style, the volume and scale also should keep unity with the whole community. In the style design, colour is a most flexible, least restricted and very effective element. It should reflect local characteristics and echo with the overall tone of the community.

'The materials used are seeking to respond appropriately to each different space and activity to be developing in the building. We have avoided excessive use of materials, the austerity and simplicity being key to achieving a unified global image. Externally the building is coated with a ventilated facade cladding polymer concrete, thanks to its high thermal inertia and black color, allows to accumulate heat in a cold and humid climate such as is the city of Vitoria-Gasteiz.

We have used a single formal language where the colour and height of the different rooms has helped to adapt each room to use. In any case the building does not look to segregate the spaces according to different uses, but all global container behaves identifiable by all kinds of users.'
(ACXT Architects, Ibaiondo Civic Centre)

The expression of architecture art mainly get through the ingenious combination between space and shape, good proportional relationship between the whole and the parts, proper treatment of colour and texture instead of tedious decoration. But the use of appropriate decoration and symbols can enhance

Social Centre in Mesoiro

Community Centre Pointe-Valaine

building expressiveness, decorative use is generally limited to certain key parts and strive to cleverly combine the function and structure of the building. Further thoughts are also needed in some detail design to add to the shape processing a certain sense of depth.

The Latrobe Valley has a deeply ingrained duality between the industrial complex of the state's electricity generators, and more traditional rural pursuits such a beef and dairy farming. The new community building sits within this industrial/rural duality, and recognises the play of other similar dynamics like suburban/rural, with the site located on the rural outskirts of Traralgon, and the ever present duality of an age-specific neighbourhood alongside its more amorphous sibling, the typical suburb. The former is defined by age, whilst the latter is shaped by more fluid socio-economic forces.

These dualities a drawn out in a number of different ways. The industrial/rural dichotomy takes shape in the use of strong, muscular forms facing the outside world, with the inner face offering a more inviting enclosed courtyard. The suburban/rural dynamic can also be found in this inner/ outer character. Whilst age is prescribed for the residents, there is no such prescription for the architecture, and the building seeks a more universal appeal. Engagement with the outside community is encouraged through its offering of café, bar, restaurant and function room.

Siting is conceived to activate and address the planned village green, and the green has been located to protect two ancient redgum trees that stand at the demographic centre of the village. The building is orientated to northwards, opening out onto planned lawn bowls and bocce greens, whilst sheltering the courtyard from strong prevailing winds from nearby farmland.

The village is designed as a permeable grid, and the building aligns itself with this grid, defined by two main axes – eastwest and north-south. These are expressed (at ground and 1st floors) by linear halls that create a sense of the infinite through sight lines extending beyond into the

Above 2: Community Centre Pointe-Valaine

landscape. The main entry is positioned to divide the building into a public west wing, with bar and restaurant, and a more private east wing with library, doctors rooms and pool.

Externally, materials oscillate from the industrial scale and finish of the metal clad upper floor, to materials of a more residential feel. The building consciously meets the ground with either brick veneer or cement sheet cladding, helping to calibrate the building with its surrounding village. Internally, a palette of timber veneer, painted plasterboard and polished concrete is used to suggest on the one hand a warm and inviting clubhouse, and on the other, a modern public building. Timber framed residential-style construction and moderate glazing area minimise building cost and maximise environmental outcomes. A complex building has been delivered on a very tight budget, whilst achieving energy efficiency levels that are well above standards.

(Adam Dettrick Architect Pty Ltd, Dalkeith Heights Community Building)

4.3 Design Concept of Coexistence with the Environment

Man is the subject, the building and its surrounding environment is the object, these two have a dynamic integration. With the help of ecological aesthetics, the relationship between man and nature, between man and environment can be studied as an ecosystem and an organic integrity. It is neither to study man without the natural environment nor study the natural environment without man. Only by achieving harmonious coexistence of man and the natural environment can the goal of being healthy, natural and harmonious be realised.

The proportion of culture ingredients in centre design should be taken seriously. The centre should take the culture as a main part, to improve cultural quality and quality of life. Green and healthy cultural theme helps to get rid of the hustle and bustle, in order to back to nature. In addition to the traditional cultural connotation, it can also give new meaning to the community.

Above 3: Maison du Chemin de l'île Community House

The physical manifestation of this objective is the day centre, which was based at the Lebenshilfe's headquarters in Brachtergasse together with the full-time assisted living unit. Despite several additions, the capacity of these premises was exhausted, and so an invited architectural competition was held. The task was to build a new day centre on a nearby disused allotment site. The new centre was to serve as a place for people to come together at different levels. In this first-prize-winning design, Ederer and Haghirian therefore apply the fundamental creed of "self-confident integration" to the concept of their architecture, too.

The location is one of the most important things to operate a successful community centre. A community centre has to be open to its neighbourhood. The location is very important. A community centre has to be in a residential area, not in an outlying district.

We wanted to make our building timeless. The community centre should nobody unsettle. It's very important to use codes, that can be read by everyone. Where do I come into the building? Where I am allowed to go, where is it forbidden? These things have to be told by the building, not a information sign.

The functions are arranged circular. The rooms can be combined but we can also separate parts

Maison du Chemin de l'île Community House

of a room. Synergic effects can be developed because of different functions using one space. So we can save space and money.

Costs are always a problem in designing community centres. We solved them in using simple materials. To economize we built a very compact structure. As a traditional building material in Austria we are using wood. This material is characterized by its warm and positive charisma and its haptic qualities. For energy-saving reasons the structure is compact built.
(EDERER + HAGHIRIAN ARCHITEKTEN ZT-OG, Lebenshilfe Weiz Centre)

References:
[1] http://en.wikipedia.org/wiki/Community_centre
[2] & [3] Landcom. (2008). Community Centre Guidelines. Sydney: Landcom
[4] Yan Yili, Discuss the Chamber Design, Chinese and Overseas Architecture, 7th volume 2008 (Cannot contact with the author)

#	Project	Enlargement	Swimming Pool	Sports Centre	Children	Library	Stage	Exhibition	Multipurpose Room	Canteen	Courtyard	Religion	Senior
01	West Vancouver Community Centre	●	●	●	●				●				
02	Huis Van Droo			●	●				●				
03	Ontwerp MFA Kulturhus Laag-Soeren			●	●	●			●				
04	Cultural and Community Centre in Bergem						●						
05	Social Centre in Mesoiro				●				●		●		
06	Batesford Reserve Community Centre								●				
07	Can Ramis Community Centre and Multipurpose Building								●	●			
08	Community Centre, Zeilsheim						●		●		●	●	
09	Sōmeru Community Centre					●	●		●		●		
10	Centennial Community Centre	●	●	●									
11	Killarney Ice Rink Community Centre	●	●										
12	Community Centre, Gersonsvej								●		●		
13	Laurimar Community Centre					●			●		●		
14	Lebenshilfe Weiz Centre								●		●		
15	Beit-Halochem		●	●					●	●	●		
16	Dalkeith Heights Community Building			●			●		●	●	●		
17	Community Centre Pointe-Valaine			●			●		●	●			
18	The Culture Yard	●											
19	Temple Sinai Community Centre	●				●	●			●	●	●	
20	Community Centre Senhora da Boa Nova				●	●			●		●	●	
21	Maison du Chemin de L'île Community House				●				●		●		●
22	Centre of Social Services in Montealto				●				●				●
23	Moonee Valley Community Centre			●		●	●		●		●		
24	Ibaiondo Civic Centre		●		●		●		●				

049

design of community centre

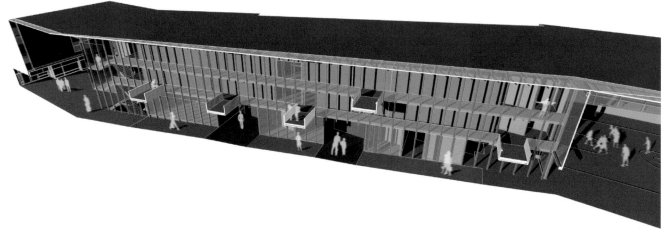

Section

West Vancouver Community Centre

Architects:
Hughes Condon Marler Architects
Location: West Vancouver, Canada
Project area: 7,639m²
Project year: 2009
Photographs: © Hubert Kang
Award: Lieutenant Governor
of British Columbia Awards for
Architecture 2010; SAB Canadian
Green Building Award 2010

The West Vancouver Community Centre involved a set of ambitious design goals. The client wished to consolidate a number of disparate facilities, to provide a front door to their recreation campus, and to take an aggressive approach to social health and environmental innovation.

The technical and administrative challenges of this project came to define the Centre's role in West Vancouver's distinctly West Coast social fabric. This is a culture that enjoys a strong tradition of both civic activity and physical wellness. The preeminent architectural elements in the project, the three-storey atrium and the circulation spine,

reflect these traditions as followed: The atrium, as both a transparent, welcoming gateway and the connective tissue between the new Community Centre and an existing Aquatic Centre, allows multiple readings. It is a formal gathering space with views to the Great Lawn and mountains beyond, as well as a casual passageway between buildings. Its scale is decidedly civic and it provides genuine public space that is flexible and stimulating. The building's luminous three-storey circulation spine works as the building's primary artery, linking gymnasiums, fitness rooms and wellness clinics both physically and visually. Articulated along the centre's

1. Day view of courtyard façade
2. Night view of courtyard façade
3. Day view of courtyard façade

length, the spine, with its operable skylights, helps drive sunlight and fresh air deep into the building. Colourful bridges on the upper levels offer casual moments of pause and opportunities for social interaction.

For anticipating LEED® Gold certification, West Vancouver Community Centre incorporates a number of sustainable design strategies including geothermal ground source system, shared energy systems, natural ventilation, day-lighting, re-use of structural elements, recycled/sensitive materials and storm water retention. The project represents a dynamic new approach to community centre design. Building upon the architectural legacy of West

Coast Modernism, the project looks boldly towards the future, while revitalizing an important civic site. The building has already become the social heart of the community.

Concept

3

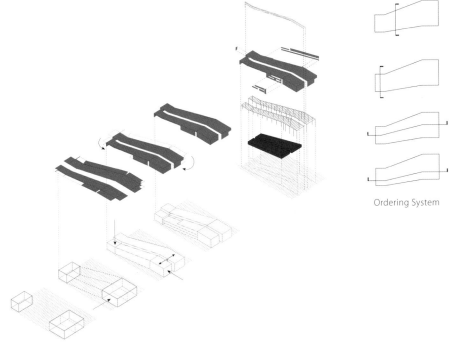

Ordering System

4. Night view of the façade
5. The main lobby
6. The entrance

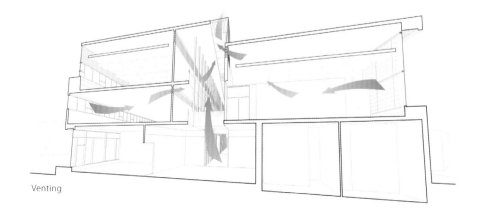

Venting

5

6

10. The inner courtyard
11. Outside the children centre
12. The media centre

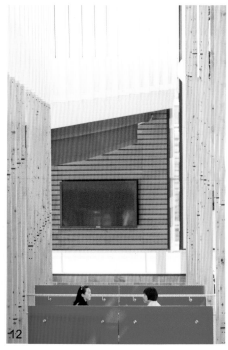

Main Floor Plan:
1. Atrium
2. Multi-purpose room
3. Meeting room
4. Child-minding
5. Children's activity
6. Games room
7. Changerooms
8. Community health
9. Multi-purpose gym
10. Dynamic movement
11. Existing Aquatic Centre
12. South plaza / entry
13. Great lawn
14. Fountain
15. Multi-purpose patio
16. Existing Seniors Centre
17. Seniors entry
18. North plaza / entry
19. Skylights to Parking /Band
20. W-shape play area
21. Youth outdoor area
22. Existing tennis courts

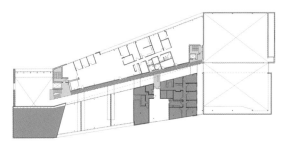

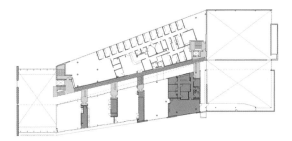

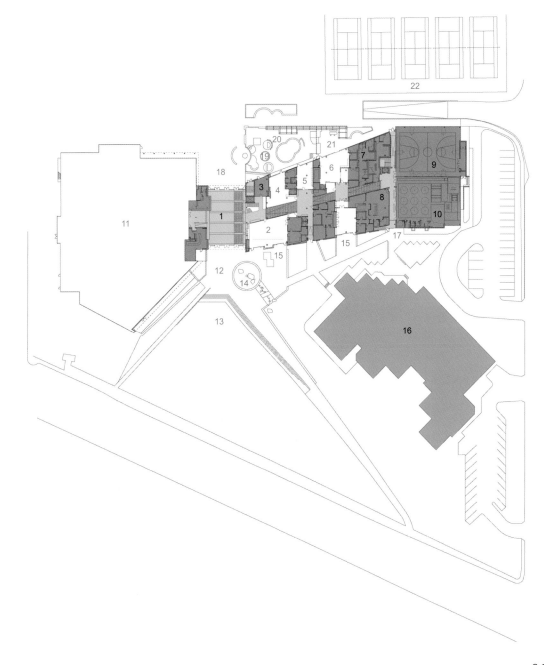

Laurimar Community Centre

Architects:
Croxon Ramsay
Location:
Whittlesea, Melbourne, Australia
Project year:
2009
Photographs:
© Courtesy of Croxon Ramsay

The new Community Centre at Laurimar is a multi-functional facility that will support a range of children's services and community activities. With the close proximity of the town centre and primary school, the Centre will provide for much needed services and community spaces in the area.

The Laurimar Community Activity Centre will create an integrated hub for all generations and provide resources for community activities. This is supported by a integrated model of service provision. Central to the design of the Community Centre is the provision of environmentally sustainable design. The ESD initiatives include natural ventilation, low VOC materials for improved indoor air quality, high efficiency mechanical systems. The extensive use of internal thermal mass and high performance building envelope means that the building internal temperature is maintained with minimal heating and cooling. The building management system monitors the internal temperatures and lighting control for best energy efficiency and incorporates user feedback.

1

1. Entrance
2. East elevation

North Elevation

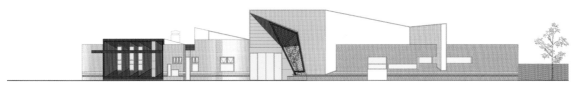

East Elevation

South Elevation

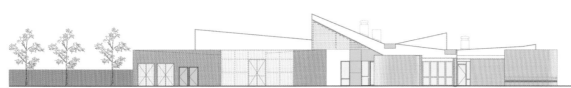

West Elevation

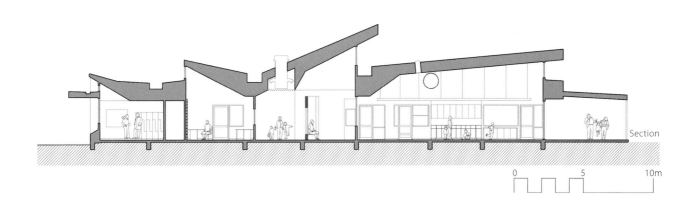

Section

0   5   10m

3. Children's play area
4, 5. Office & atrium

Floor Plan:
1. Children's room
2. Kitchen
3. Office
4. Foyer
5. Atrium
6. Consult
7. Meeting
8. Community courtyard
9. Waiting
10. Children's play area
11. Staff

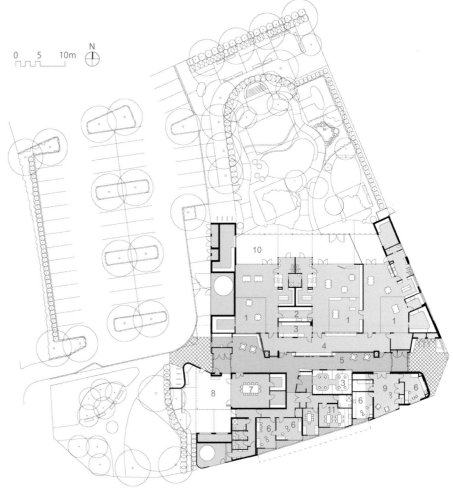

Huis Van Droo

Architects:
Johan De Wachter Architecten
Location:
Duiven, the Netherlands
Project area:
1,650m²
Project year:
2012
Photographs:
© JDWA –
Johan De Wachter Architects

Social community centre Huis van Droo (lit. House of Droo) is located in the heart of the master plan for Droo-South area in Duiven (the Netherlands) that envisions the renewal of this entire neighbourhood. JDWA, the design team of Huis van Droo, is also responsible for the preparation of this master plan, as well as the design of the communal garden — Tuin van Droo — surrounding Huis van Droo and the connection to the adjacent nursing home. Incorporating these different scales in the design process, from small to large, made it possible to improve the quality of architecture and the public space and to ensure an optimal integration of sustainability measures for the entire project.

Interactive process — From the beginning of the draft master plan the architects have

been extensively working together with the current residents of the neighbourhood, the new users (HMOs) and the future users of Huis van Droo. In interactive sessions, they outlined the layout for the renewal of Droo-South. This method was continued well into the building design phase of Huis van Droo as well as for the design of the Tuin van Droo.

Shared use and dual use — To realise the versatile programme (housing, care housing, primary care, sports, childcare, community facilities) within the confines of the renewal statement, there was a real need to efficiently target and assign the available space. It was necessary to share both indoor and outdoor spaces. This way the plan could retain sufficient light and

1. Building façade and surroundings
2. Entrance of neighbourhood lounge
3. View across pond
4. Neighbourhood lounge
5. Staircase
6. Spacious dojo
7. Detailing inner façade
8. Central gymnasium

air and only then would the public space really remain available to play, meet and relax.

Droo-South:
sustainable neighbourhood — The three architects responsible for the architecture in Droo-South have continually tuned their design, programme and building typology paying full attention to sustainability in all its aspects and scales. As for sustainability measures for Huis van Droo; JDWA in collaboration with various consultants made an extra effort. The building envelope (steel & timber frame construction) and technical measures (cold-heat storage, solar collectors, heat pumps, etc.) are perfectly matched. Due to their involvement with the master plan it was possible to improve the building development with technical systems that they could share with the other new buildings. Thus the whole system of cold-heat storage is shared with the adjacent nursing home, increasing the efficiency of the systems' usage greatly.

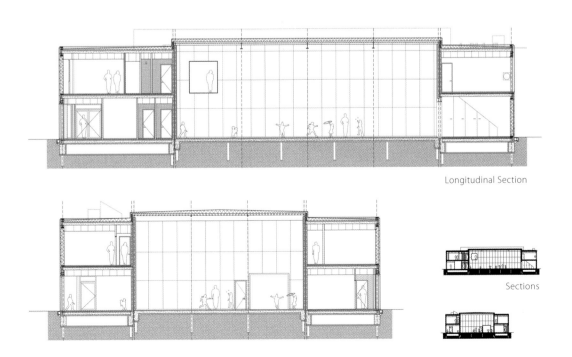

Longitudinal Section

Sections

Inner Lining:
1. Inner lining
- Hardwood vertical battens, 43×43mm
- Core-to-core distance 100mm
- Plywood backing, 12mm
- Flame retardant finish
2. Anodized aluminium curtain wall
3. Multibladed insulating tinted glass
4. Calcium silicate masonry
5. Anchor
6. Anodized aluminium plate
7. Outer cladding
- Hardwood vertical battens,
  43×43mm c.t.c.100mm
- Framework beveled for drainage
- Flame retardant hardwood
- Mounted on subframe (timber frame)
  with stainless steel L-profile
8. Timber frame construction; inside>outside
- 12.5 mm Fermacell
- 12mm OSB (Oriented Strand Board)
- Vapour barrier
- Timber frame
- Mineral wool insulation; Rc value acc EPN report
- Foil, water-repelent, open to diffusion
9. Fibre cement board
- 30mm wooden framework with insect grids
- Bostic profiles
- 8mm Cembrit-Metro
- Screws with coloured heads

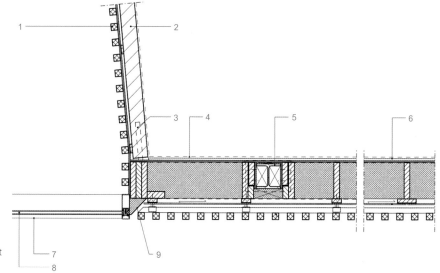

Ground Floor Plan:
1. Paramedic function
2. Technique
3. Entry waiting
4. Physic
5. Sports hall

First Floor Plan:
1. Children cluster
2. Lounge area
3. Ward
4. Sports hall

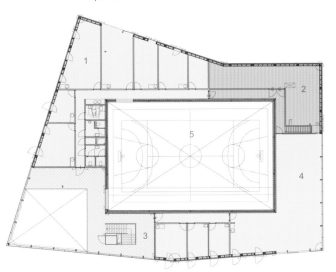

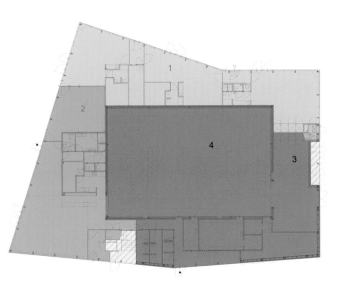

1

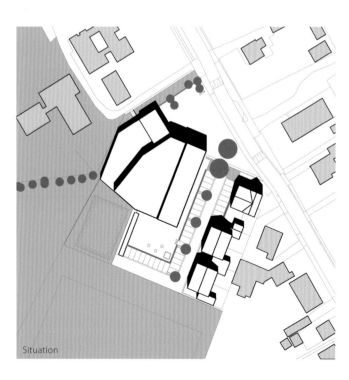

Situation

Ontwerp MFA Kulturhus Laag-Soeren

Architects:
Mark Koopman, KAW architects
and advisors
Location:
Laag Soeren, the Netherlands
Project area:
2,100m²
Project year:
2009
Photographs:
© Gerard van Beek Fotografie

The decrease of the number of inhabitants and the ageing of inhabitants left cause social problems in rural areas in the Netherlands. The small village Laag Soeren struggles with these demographic changes, and leaves the village with no health and care facilities as a result. The new cultural centre is there to turn this development around.

This centre provides a base for various social organisations in the area. It houses the village school, a nursery, a community house, a daytime activity centre for people with disabilities, a general practitioner and a number of sports clubs. Together with these different users, the architects developed a common vision for the cultural centre, in which collaboration and

common use of space was the key point. What is special about this concept, is that the clients of the daytime activity centre actually manage various services in the cultural centre, like the reception, the store and the bar.

The programme comprises classrooms, a gymnasium, day care rooms, workshops for the activity centre, consulting rooms, offices, a store, a grand café and multifunctional spaces. This programme is arranged around a multifunctional space located in the heart of the building. This area functions as a covered village square, and is the location where different users meet each other. The space, that can be enlarged with the gymnasium, is shaped as an amphitheatre and can host small and

1. Front façade and courtyard
2. Front façade and courtyard (night view)
3. Back façade gymnasium

large events alike. The rooms that can be used by other tenants are located directly next to this square. The more private rooms are in the back of the building.

The interior is a beautiful mix of homely and light and airy. The many vistas provide views on the luscious landscape. The materialisation gives the interior a natural and modest appearance.

Laag Soeren is a little village with low buildings bordering the nature park De Veluwezoom. The architects' main motivation was to incorporate the building in the vulnerable surrounding without bringing harm to it.

The sculptural form of the building follows its surrounding, with the bending of the façade decreasing the buildings' mass. The materialisation of the exterior is natural and robust. The brickwork and concrete give it a timeless appearance. A spectacular cantilever marks the entrée of the building, and a built-in bench makes the transition to the human scale. The transparency of the building allows the spectator to view through the building to the landscape behind.

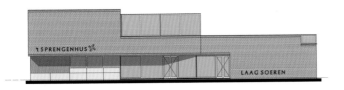

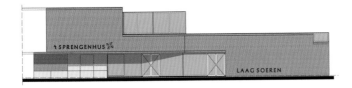

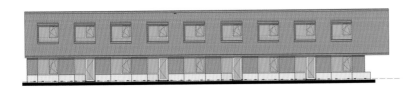

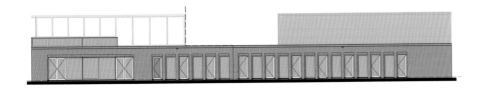

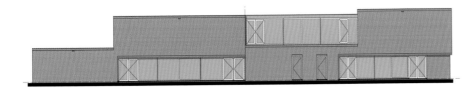

Elevations

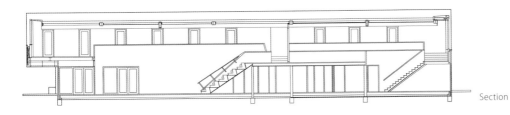

Section

4. Central multifunctional hall
5. Gymnasium
6. Hallway Primary School
7. Library

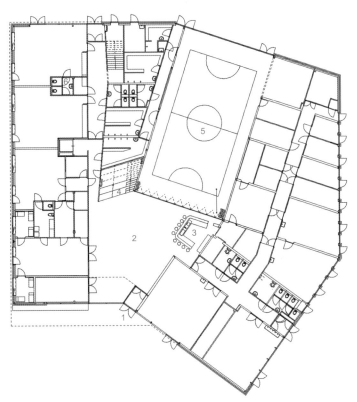

Ground Floor Plan:
1. Main entrance
2. Hall
3. Reception
4. Village square
5. Gymnasium
6. Restroom

1

Cultural and Community Centre in Bergem

Architects:
BRUCK + WECKERLE
ARCHITEKTEN
Location:
Bergem, Luxembourg
Project area:
2,400m²
Project year:
2011
Photographs:
© Lukas Roth, BWA

A new cultural centre was to replace the dilapidated community centre in the heart of the village of Bergem. A condition of the commission was that clubs could continue their activities in the existing building until the new one was ready. Dominating the remaining free space on the plot, which borders a green zone, was a majestic walnut tree.

Bruck + Weckerle Architekten felt that this tree, sheltering its meadow for over 80 years, was such a feature of the village of Bergem that it deserved to be retained and displayed to its best advantage. They

recognised the scope offered by this symbolic tree, when allied to subtlety of design, for creating a unique meeting point that would not only reconcile the natural and cultural worlds but also architecturally enrich the core of the village.

The design concept comprises a low, rectangular structure covering the entire remainder of the plot. Where the walnut tree stands, a semicircular recess is scooped out of that stark geometry – creating a transitional zone between indoors and outdoors. The building

2

1. Façade
2. Street elevation

appears to welcome visitors with open arms and to embrace the walnut tree.

The welcoming stance of the semicircular inner courtyard contributes to the character of the building and draws the visitor to the heart of it. A curved wall, panelled in walnut, sweeps round to create a single uninterrupted space that surrounds the entire inner courtyard and leads to the main hall. The wall facing onto the tree is wholly glass, including glass doors that can be opened in fine weather to give access to the courtyard.

This spatial organisation offers many different ways of using the space. All the ancillary rooms are located behind the curved wall. The falling contour allows

natural light in the basement, where the spaces for delivery are situated. They can be accessed any time from behind the building, independently from events and visitors. Also the clubrooms and the entire logistics are located in the basement. The building meets the modern requirements with respect to ecology, engineering and building technology (green roof, rain water usage, ground-coupled heat exchanger etc.).

The main hall is of a simple, harmoniously constituted design that is at the same time self-contained yet open to the surrounding landscape. The space can be divided through a mobile partition wall, allowing the different atmospheres from family living room

to high-tech multi-functionality. The ceiling and the panels between the windows are finished in walnut veneer and decorated with a pattern of perforations especially designed for this room and its acoustic demands.

As an external expression of the building's cultural role and its restrained festivity, a stylised red stage curtain serves as a metaphor for celebration, community and culture. Cast in concrete, a freeze-frame image, it nevertheless seems to move back and forth as the light brightens or dims in time to the swaying branches. The windows are vertical bands of glass, splitting the curtain into strips as if it had simply been pushed to a side.

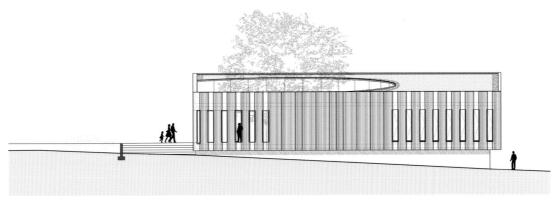

Street Elevation

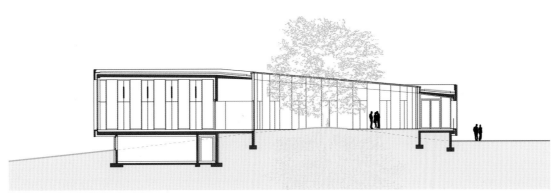

Longitudinal Section

Situation Plan

083

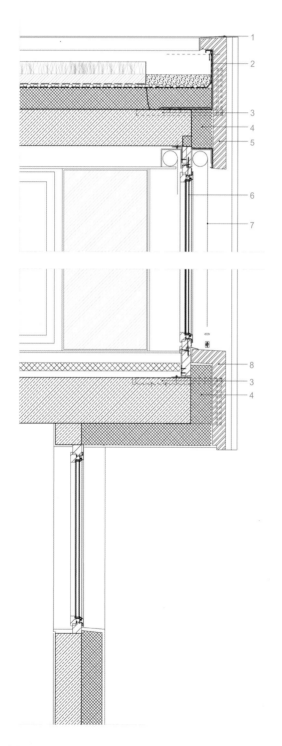

Vertical Section Detail - C.3, C.4 (Left):
1. Aluminium profile
2. L-profile of sheet steel, 5 mm
3. Recess in the concrete for HALFEN BRA-NJ
4. Insulation, 160 mm
5. Precast concrete element C.3, 100 mm
6. Sun protection glass, 6 mm
7. Sun shading
8. Precast concrete element C.4, 100 mm

Horizontal Section Detail - B.0, C.4:
1. Precast concrete element B.0, 205 mm
2. Insulation, 160 mm
3. Cast-in-place concrete, 200 mm
4. Air gap, 120 mm
5. Acoustic walnut veneered MDF panel, 19 mm
6. Precast concrete element C.4, 100 mm
7. Sun protection glass, 6 mm

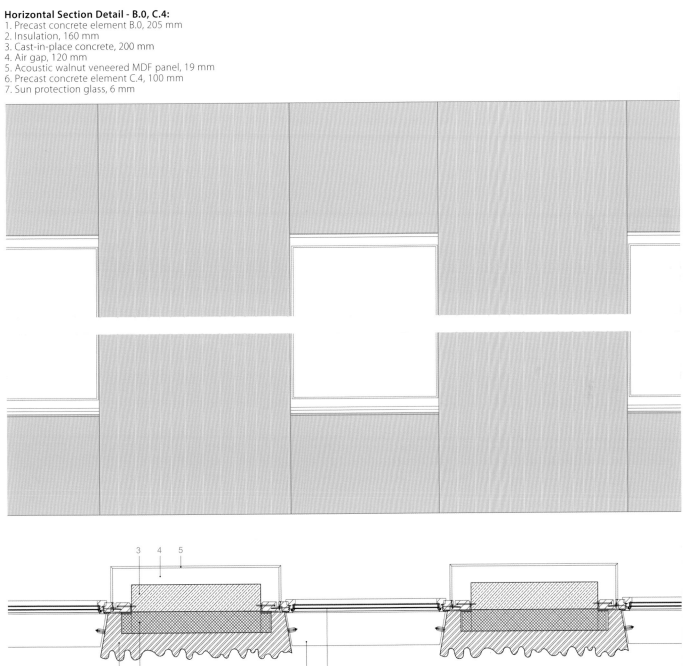

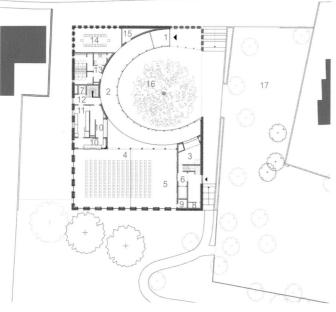

Ground Floor Plan:
1. Main entrance
2. Foyer
3. Cloakroom
4. Dividable festival room
5. Stage
6. Backstage
7. Lift
8. Stage technology
9. Sliding partition storage
10. Beverage counter
11. Kitchen
12. Access secondary rooms
13. Restrooms
14. Conference
15. Cleaning room
16. Existing tree
17. Parking

4. Atrium
5. Foyer
6. Entrance
7. Conference

7

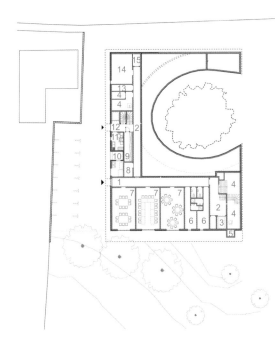

Basement Plan:
1. Basement entrance
2. Corridor
3. Lift
4. Technical room
5. Shaft for ground-coupled
   heat exchanger
6. Changing room for artists
7. Club room
8. Beer cellar
9. Cold room
10. Waste
11. Dishwashing
12. Access secondary rooms
13. Cleaning room
14. Storage
15. House service connection

Social Centre in Mesoiro

Architects:
Naos Architecture
(Santiago González & Miguel Porras)
Location:
A Coruña, Spain
Project area:
2,099m²
Project year
2011
Photographs:
© Héctor Santos-Diez

The building was designed to be a social and services centre in a neighbourhood with a high population growth rates in recent years. It is destined to use of the people in Mesoiro, A Coruña, a area with 7,900 inhabitants.

It includes a gathering place for neighbours and the cultural equipment: multi-use rooms, auditorium, reading room, play room, others spaces for children and adults and office works.

The programme develops in a single floor at ground level. The building and rooms are entered through a front interior courtyard that is directly connected to the hall and auditorium. This courtyard is protected place from prevailing winds of the zone and

it serves as an outside play area for children, but joined to the interior play room.

The building is arranged into three volumes. The greater height volume has an entrance hall and multi-purpose room. The next volume houses a play room, social offices, reading room, multipurpose room, dressing rooms, toilets and plant rooms. The distribution of the edifice proposes to create a large open space in the centre. The space can be divided according to needs of exhibitions or events it houses, using movable panels.

In this way, this possibility of distribution means an improvement in the use of the building, connecting the two spaces:

1. The building was designed to be a social and services centre and is arranged into three volumes
2. Main entrance
3. Lateral façade

entrance hall and multipurpose room, and the central courtyard too. This large area offers great versatility and flexibility to the usage of building that can change frequently. It also has a detachable stage with a practical system that takes advantage the auditorium as other multipurpose room more.

On both sides of the central volume, two pieces were constructed with functional purpose. The play room oriented to the courtyard and the meeting place for elder people.

The design of a building destined for public use requires a practical organization in its distribution, accesses, itineraries and rooms. It allows ability to circulate and

communicate unimpeded. The Civic and Social Centre of Mesoiro was designed in a single floor, which prevents vertical circulations and allows its use in a most comfortable way.

One of the aspects is the accessibility for people with disabilities, so were step-free spaces, both width and height dimensions. The possibility to move freely within the space allows the interrelationship between areas of public without interference.
At the same time, in the case of Mesoiro building, the patio of access becomes a large indoor lobby where directly accessing the Auditorium and protected from the prevailing winds in this area.

A building with energetic requirements

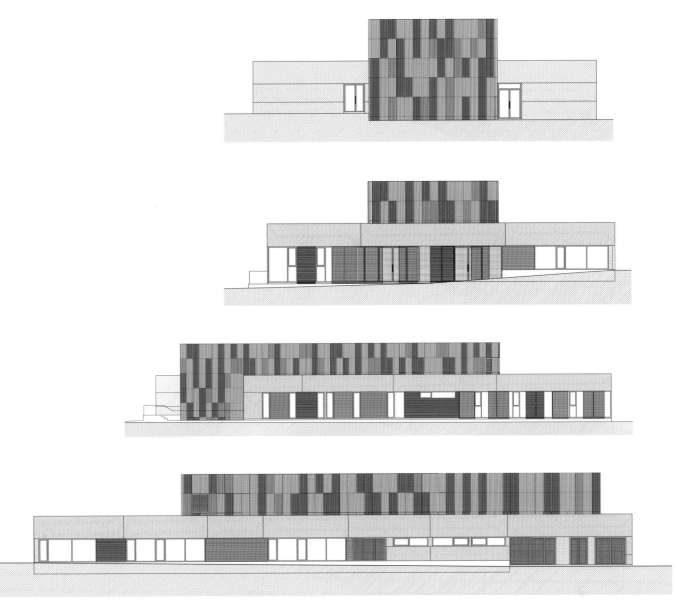

Elevations

indicated by the budget has to be designed under the concept of making good use of the environment energetic resources. Also, the design of the materials should be optimized, giving it durability and low maintenance cost, with the aim of easing and making possible the future rentability of this investment.

-Design of open building, connected with the neighbourhood and accessible to those who will use the building in different ways.
- The lighting and ventilation of the building is natural in many rooms, accesses and itineraries.
- Area for use by children is linked to the yard for your enjoyment on sunny days and is sized for children
- The dimensions of the spaces, both in height and in width, allow the free passage of people
- The circulations are designed without interference, as a measure of protection and security both in the reading room, children's room, offices and auditorium
- The pavements are non-slip and ready for continuous use
- Offices of used for administrative purposes are grouped to one side of the building to help a private use

4-6. The building and rooms are entered through a front interior
courtyard that is directly connected to the hall and auditorium.
This courtyard is protected place from prevailing winds of the
zone and it serves as an outside play area for children, but
joined to the interior play room.

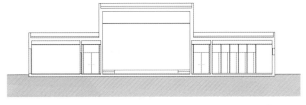

Sections

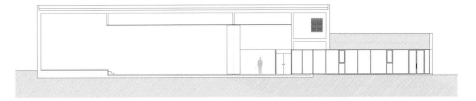

Ground Floor Plan:
1. Entrance
2. Multi-purpose room
3. Multi-purpose room
4. Play room
5. Offices
6. Toilets
7. Dressing room
8. Plant room

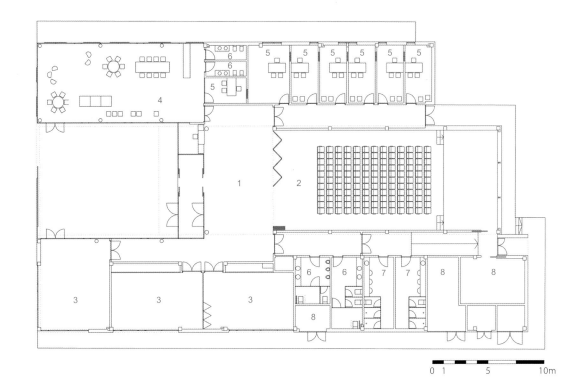

0 1 5 10m

7-8. The greater height volume has an entrance hall and multi-purpose room. The space can be divided according to needs of exhibitions or events it houses, using movable panels.
9. On both sides of the central volume, two pieces were constructed with functional purpose. The play room oriented to the courtyard and the meeting place for the old.

1

Batesford Reserve
Community Centre

Architects:
Croxon Ramsay P/L
Location:
Monash, Australia
Project year:
2009
Photographs:
© Rhiannon Slatter

The Batesford Reserve Community Centre provides the opportunity to develop and extend much needed services and facilities to the community in the Ashwood area of the City of Monash.

This multipurpose facility also sets best practice environmental design benchmarks. The ESD initiatives include an innovative ventilation and cooling system which incorporates a sub-floor cooling system and thermal chimneys. The extensive use of internal thermal mass and high performance building envelope means that the building internal temperature is maintained with minimal heating and cooling. The building management system monitors the internal temperatures and lighting control for best energy efficiency while low VOC and recycled materials improve the indoor air quality.

The core design idea follows the principal of integration – sustainable aspects of the design are not isolated parts but, instead, exist within a deep wall section that performs several tasks simultaneously. The result is a volume that has a thick rind of exposed thermal mass, in which other sustainability systems are carved. A well-defined building in a grassy Australian suburban landscape, rather than a fussy sum of sustainable 'fascinators', is the value of this design.

3

1-2. North elevation
3. Entrance
4. South elevation

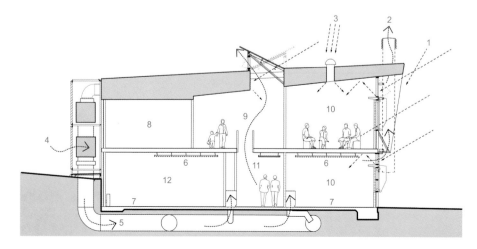

High Level Awning Windows Controlled By Bms System:
1. Roof overhang to shade in summer, allowing sun penetration in winter
2. Thermal chimney
3. Daylight
4. Evaporative system. Outdoor air intake
5. Underfloor supply air
6. Acoustic absorption and services
7. Exposed thermal mass
8. Office
9. Common area
10. Meeting
11. Foyer
12. IT lab

4

Accommodating a variety of community associations ranging from health, family and youth, employment training and senior citizen educational facilities, the building adds significantly to the domain of public facilities for the City of Monash. Its environmental systems are publicly monitored for educative interest and example.

The site is in Chadstone. It is a recreational reserve comprising a sports pavilion and oval, a basketball centre and a children's playground. The new building programme gives the reserve a richer grain as it operates largely during business hours — the

recreational peak hours being non-business. The surrounding residential neighbourhood was developed as a new (outer) residential suburb in the 1950s, on land that was once used for market gardens and farms. The reserve is a topographic brownfield of cut and fill.

The building site within the reserve marks the nexus between existing buildings and car-parking so that open space is maintained and existing connections enhanced. The materials respond to a colour palette sympathetic to the existing landscape and consistent with themes running through other council projects.

From an ESD perspective, the project is rigorous. From solar optimised sitting down to radially sawn stringybark timber cladding, the building thoroughly considers energy and waste management efficiency.

Rainwater harvesting is used not only for toilet flushing and irrigation but is a treated for use in the evaporative cooling system. Surface swales are incorporated into the landscape to maximize irrigation across the low water-use vegetation site.

5

6

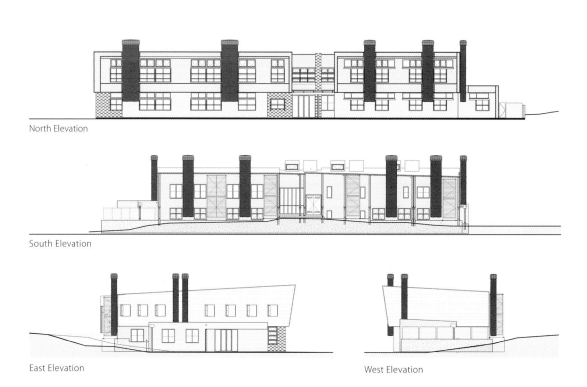

North Elevation

South Elevation

East Elevation

West Elevation

5. Detail
6. East elevation
7. Reception

8-9. Foyer
10. Meeting room

Floor plan:
1. Entry
2. Reception
3. Foyer
4. Manager
5. Store
6. Consult
7. Office
8. Kitchen
9. Meeting
10. Meeting
11. IT lab
12. Common area

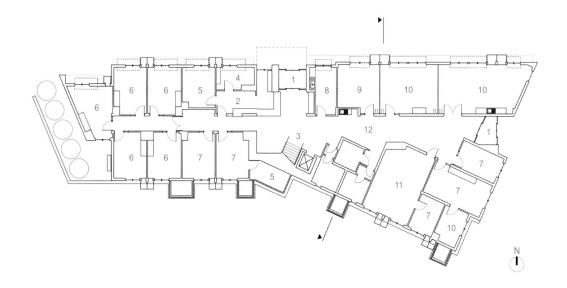

1

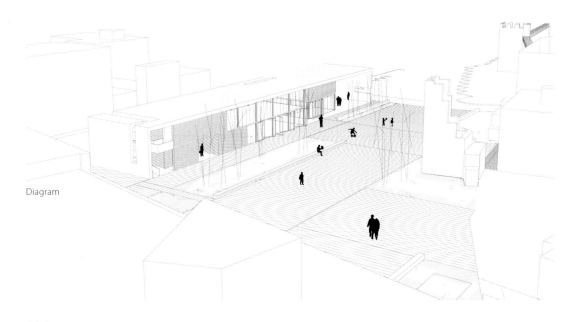

Diagram

Can Ramis Community Centre and Multipurpose Building

Architects:
pedro quero architects ltd.
Location:
Alcùdia, Majorca, Spain
Project area:
1,200m²
Construction area:
1,050m²
Project year: 2010
Photographs:
© archipress arq.& com sl

How to act against the remnants of the historic walls of Alcudia? How to intervene against the historic building began in times of James II? The reinterpretation of the walls and the symbolic environment of the place, gave the keys to solve the proposal.

The new multipurpose building replaces the existing buildings in the same position and proportion. It is conceived as a new gateway to the walled city of Alcudia, as an element that symbolizes the southern access to the site of the city. The large concrete porch below will integrate all the pieces of different applications programme by dwelling units each other to create protected areas for shade and covered outdoor waiting areas.

The proposed wooden and glass light pieces will reduce the scale of the buildings. Its disposal will enable the proposal as a filter with built-up areas and empty zones, with indoor and outdoor places, areas of shadow, subtly secrete pedestrian traffic area, forming a new square in the remains of walls and new city gate proposal. A building to be crossed, with its limits diluted, which is and goes but ordered environment that will become a large pedestrian area dotted with gardens, forming a wide gap that will dignify the wall. A place occupied only by proposing a simple furniture and neutral

2

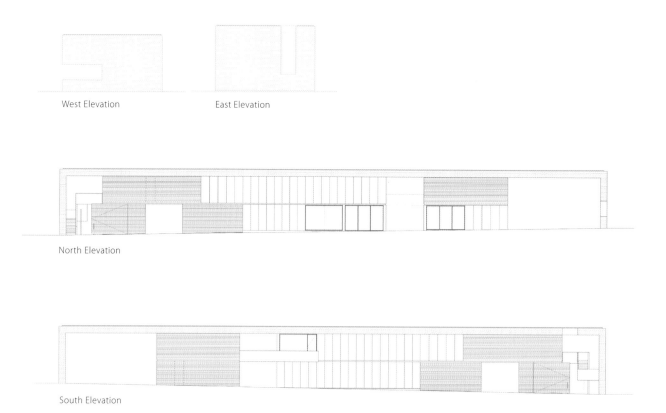

West Elevation   East Elevation

North Elevation

South Elevation

place from which to contemplate large walled debris while allowing the installation of trading posts stretching the weekly market.

... And it´ll be a new contemporary door, a reinterpreted access to the walled citadel, integrating a diverse programme in a single image, providing spaces for shadow ... who will enter visitors to the walled city of Alcudia ...

1. Main view from the new pedestrian area. The building appears as an urban filter managing relationships between two different parts in the city.
2. A main concrete structure covers all the varied programme which is finished in glass and wood. It also protects from the sunshine, providing some shadow waiting areas.

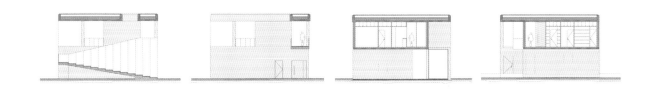

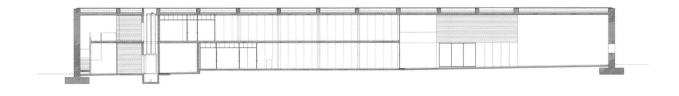

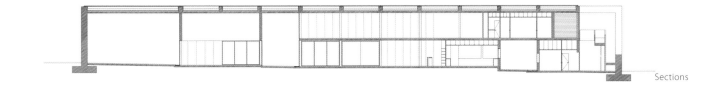

Sections

3. Side view
4. A transparent filter but a protection to the a new
   pedestrian area for the town... a vanishing bound
5-6. Exterior stairs to the upper level
7. Connection gangway in upper level
8. Interior view. Ground floor clear polyvalent area
9. Interior view. First floor clear polyvalent area
10. Ground floor aisle

7

8

9

10

General Plan:
A. Bus stop office
B. Restaurant
C. Toutist information
D. Plaza

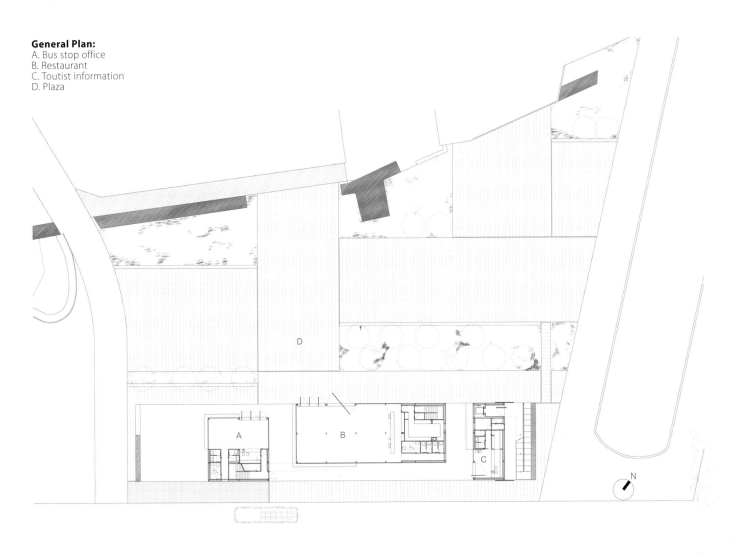

**Ground Floor Plan (Left) and
First Floor Plan (Left Below):**
1. Porch
2. Foyer
3. Restrooms
4. Office
5. Restaurant
6. Kitchen
7. Storage
8. Restrooms
9. Information
10. Restrooms
11. Clean room
12. Elevator
13. Mech.
14. Social hall
15. Office

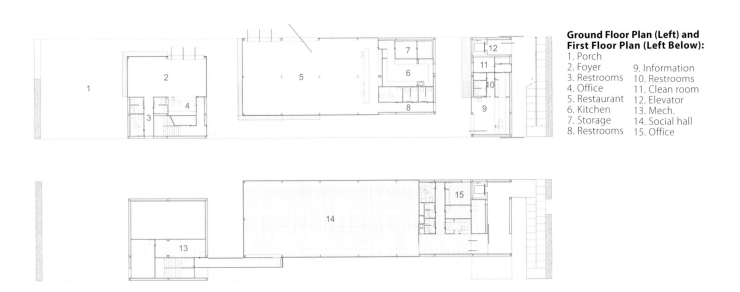

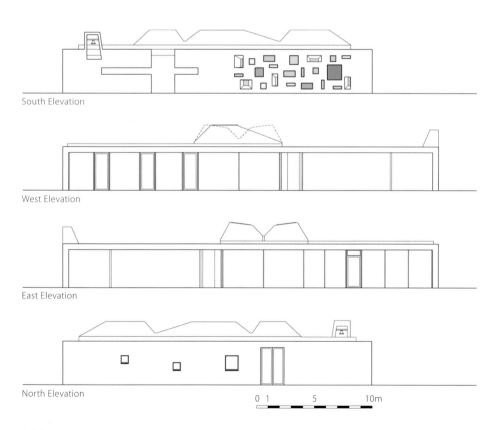

South Elevation

West Elevation

East Elevation

North Elevation

0 1   5   10m

Community Centre, Zeilsheim

Architects:
netzwerkarchitekten
Location:
Frankfurt, Germany
Project area:
2,152m²
Project year:
2011
Photographs:
© Jörg Hempel

Two conditions were essential to the development of the architect's plan: the requirement of the client to construct a building to the Passive House Standard, and the location of the property at the main development road (called Pfaff fenwiese) with heavy traffic. The annual heating requirements of the building are 15kwH/sqm only. This contributes substantially to low operating costs and resource conservation, including simple cleanability of the building, low-maintenance grounds (mainly consisting of a lawn), and good recyclability of the easy to disassemble construction and easily separable construction materials use etc. The energetic optimisation required by the Passive House Standard leads to a compact, rectangular and consistently zoned arrangement of the spatial location plan covering approximately 400 square metres. Auxiliary functions are organised alongside one corridor to the north and the connecting hall with the foyer and group rooms oriented towards the south of the property. This area can be separated by mobile partition walls, which allows for a multitude of combinations o of various rooms. Five large 'light funnels', which lead to glass skylights, form the roof off the hall and foyer. As a result, the spacious connecting hall benefits from a substantial room height combined with natural light from above and a view of the sky.

For reasons of noise control as well as passive generation of solar energy, the interior volume of the parish centre has

2

been located away from alongside the southern side of the property 'Pfaffenwiese' avenue and it's flanking high trees.

As a result, the interior volume occupies more or less the northern half of a rectangular framework made of white facing concrete, which surrounds the open spaces in front of the connecting hall. This closely associates the open spaces with the connecting hall rooms as a kind of outdoor extension: By opening the southern storey-height glass façade, the rooms and their usage can be extended towards the outside. A lawn in front of the hall, a generous wooden deck in front of the foyer/group room, a roofed area with sitting accommodation on the back of the entrance wall facing the

street, and a covered walkway offering weather protected entry to the foyer form the setting for diverse parish life completely barrier-free/ handicapped accessible.

This outdoor space in front of the building serves as an intersection leading to the public area. This space is separated from the street by a 50cm thick solid wall with openings, which provide for its sculptured appearance.

With the wide spanned open frame, a distinct type of parish centre has been created, which provides the protected space necessary for parish work while at the same time communicating its striking presence within the public space.

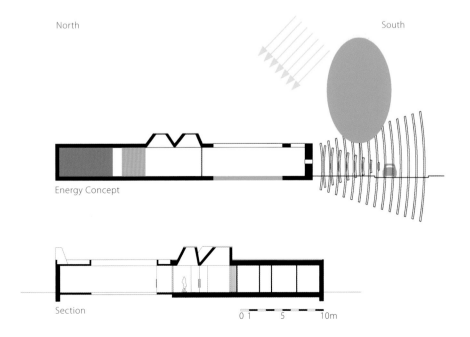

North

South

Energy Concept

Section

0 1   5   10m

4. East façade

Site Plan

0 ___ 10m

5

5. Group room
6. Church room

Ground Floor Plan:
1. Side entrance
2. Archive
3. Office
4. Group room
5. Foyer
6. Kitchen
7. Storage
8. Wardobe pram park
9. Church room
10. WC
11. Engineering room
12. Wooden deck
13. Bell tower
14. Main entrance
15. Lawn
16. Church windows

0 1   5   10m

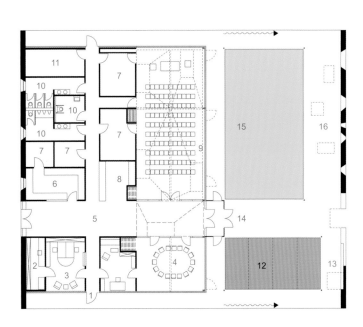

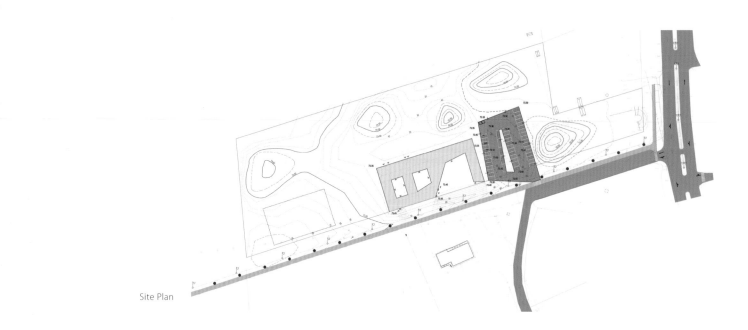
Site Plan

Sõmeru Community Centre

Architects:
Salto AB
Location:
Lääne-Viru County, Estonia
Project area:
2,144m²
Project year:
2010
Photographs:
© Karli Luik

Built according to the winning design in an architectural competition, the Sõmeru Community Centre is located just outside the North-Estonian town of Rakvere, on an open field near the highway in Sõmeru parish. Instead of erecting different buildings for their many needs, the parish decided to combine multiple functions in one single building. The multipurpose community centre houses the parish administration, a library, and a club with a 190-seat auditorium. Different heights of specific rooms create an undulating roof, under which many of the technical facilities are hidden.

The building was designed to stand apart from the existing built environment, more relating to the field surrounding it. This has been achieved by using colourful straw-like wooden beams attached to the black-and-white concrete façade. The beams are painted green, beige and dark yellow, reflecting the field changing its colour during different seasons. The same aesthetics continues in the interior, only this time the unpainted slats are hanging freely from the ceiling, creating a lively accent while moving around in draught above the jet-black walls.

1. Façade
2. Façade facing the residential area
3. The colour of the façade reflects its surroundings
4. View from the field

The single-storey building's many entwining functions are arranged compactly, with common areas in the central part, and rooms demanding more privacy surrounding them. It is possible to use the interior as one flowing space but also as separate units. There is enough room for common space, including three open courtyards, each with a specific character: the representative front yard with a fountain is meant for formal events and used mainly by the administration; the club has a more cosy one with a fireplace; and an intimate grass-covered garden with stationary plants is treated as an open-air part of the library, where visitors can sit around and read books during warmer months.

Each room in the building opens to the field or into one of the inner yards, no views are interrupted. This way the staff and visitors alike can comprehend the uniformity between the building and its surroundings.

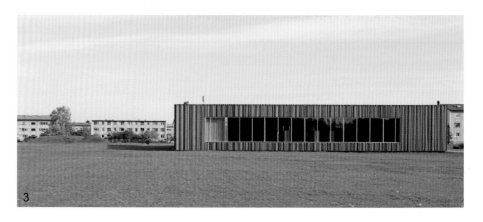

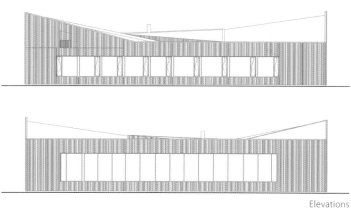

Elevations

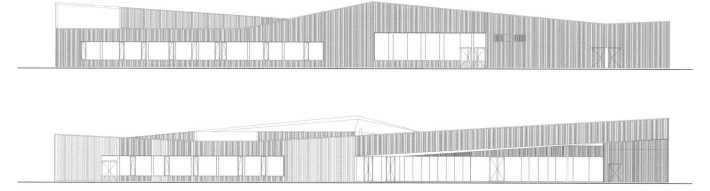

5. The undulating roof-line reflects different room heights in the interior

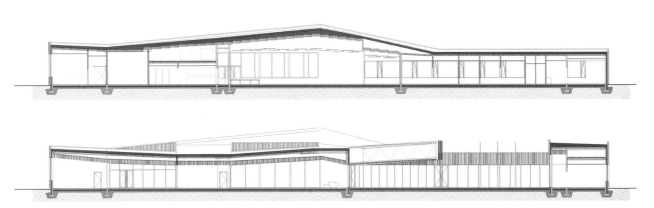

Sections

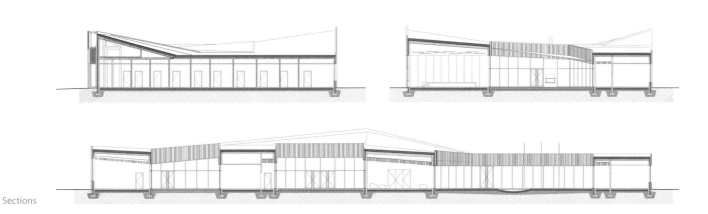

Sections

6. Library garden
7. Club garden

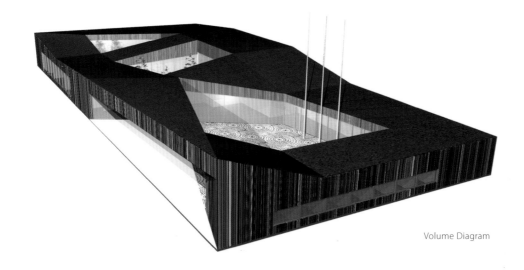

Volume Diagram

Floor Plan:
1. Parish administration's garden
2. Lobby
3. Parish administration
4. Club's garden
5. Hall
6. Hobby groups
7. Library's garden
8. Day care centre
9. Library

8. Parish administration courtyard
9. Corridor in the administration side

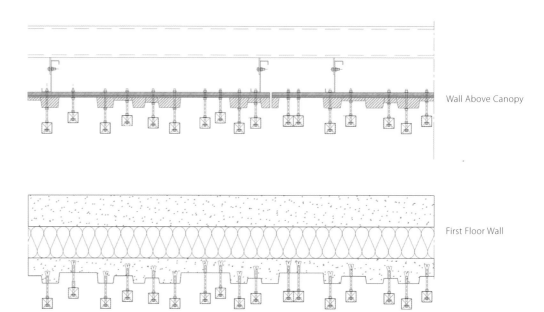

Wall Above Canopy

First Floor Wall

9

1

Centennial Community Centre

Architects:
Taylor Smyth architects
Location:
Markham, Ontario, Canada
Project area:
49,000m²
Project year: 2008
Photographs:
© Ben Rahn/A-Frame Inc.

This renovation and addition improves upon the original building while adding new programme spaces. The existing building, consisting of an arena, pool and shared lobby, presented a solid, closed face to the street with little natural light. Extensive use of transparent and translucent glazing on the addition makes the new building more inviting, enticing approaching visitors with views of the activities occurring inside and affording abundant natural light for users.

Located in the centre of Markham Town the project is the recreational centre for the whole community. Additions to the existing building include new entries, fitness club, gymnasium and interior Bocce facility. The existing pool change rooms were renovated, along with administrative offices and the lobby. The existing parking lot was redesigned to create a more urban forecourt/drop off to the building with a public plaza animated by benches, lighting and planting.

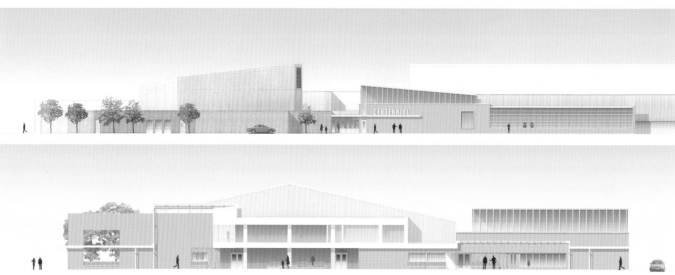

A new glass enclosed interior ramp from the ground to the second floor is a feature of the main façade of the building and celebrates accessibility. The upper part of the ramp projects out from the building, providing views of users moving between the floors. The adjacent fitness club is enclosed on two sides with a glass wall consisting of translucent glazing interspersed with slots of clear glass and one large 'sky view' picture window. A tall wall of yellow glazed block runs the length of the main interior street/corridor as an orientation device, projecting out into the public plaza. Along it runs a long canopy, welcoming and providing shelter. Inside, many new openings provide views from circulation spaces, both into activity areas and between adjacent activity areas.

The building qualified for a $60,000 CBIP grant for energy saving measures. A series of up-front additions to the building programme will provide annual operating savings of $70,000 with a payback period of approximately 3 years.

1. View of gymnasium
2. Rear entry
3. Side view of centre
4. Reception corner
5. Foyer

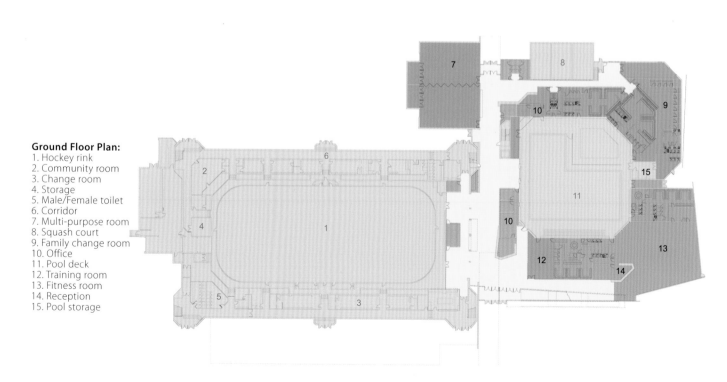

Ground Floor Plan:
1. Hockey rink
2. Community room
3. Change room
4. Storage
5. Male/Female toilet
6. Corridor
7. Multi-purpose room
8. Squash court
9. Family change room
10. Office
11. Pool deck
12. Training room
13. Fitness room
14. Reception
15. Pool storage

6. View down ramp outside
7. View up ramp
8. Gym

1

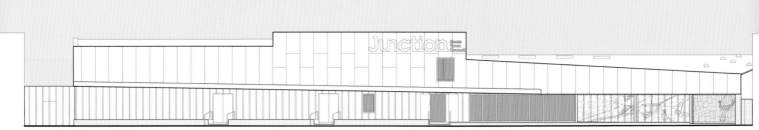

West Elevation

0　2　5　　10m

Killarney Ice Rink Community Centre

Architects:
Acton Ostry Architects
Location:
Vancouver, Canada
Project area:
3,716m²
Project year:
2009
Photographs:
© Nic Lehoux

The Killarney Ice Rink + Lobby project is a replacement of an existing ice rink and lobby at the Killarney Community Centre in Vancouver that is comprised of a swimming pool facility, an ice rink, a gymnasium, and other activity spaces.

The renewal of the Killarney Community Centre complex improved access to the facility in order that it may continue to serve its vital role as a key social hub of the Killarney neighbourhood. The arena was designed to act as a short-track speed skating training venue for the 2010 Winter Games. After the completion of the Games, the international-size ice surface was converted to an NHL-sized rink with seating for 250 spectators to use by the community.

The form, massing and materials reflect those of the existing facility to create a harmonious, unified expression for the entire community centre complex. The roof slope over the new rink mirrors the slope of the roof of the existing pool facility, thereby creating a focus to the main entry and lobby. Generous canopies

1. Entrance
2. Façade
3. Entry lobby

are provided at main entries to provide shelter and to serve as transition zones between the interior and exterior.

The arena is constructed of tilt-up precast concrete accented with masonry veneer and standing seam metal cladding to match materials used at the existing swimming pool building. The lobby is constructed with a combination of structural steel, glulam beams and extensive floor to ceiling glazing. Blue, violet and fuchsia hues of coloured glass vividly animate the crisp, frosty white of the rink interior.

The skater lounge accommodates public functions and social activities when not occupied for rink use. Administration offices take advantage of borrowed natural light and facilitate public interaction with staff via the adjacent lobby. The lobby is designed to accommodate public events, activities and gatherings.

New landscaping is concentrated around the perimeter of the ice rink and lobby. An outdoor terrace, located adjacent to the main entry approach incorporates benches and shade trees and can be used as an outdoor room to support

community activities. A large landscape berm and trees located to the west of the ice rink serve to anchor the rink to the land in a manner complementary to the neighbouring swimming pool.

To achieve LEED Gold certification, a key design strategy was employed to take advantage of the inherent synergies that exist between the exchange of heating and cooling capabilities associated with the refrigeration system of the new ice rink. Excess heat generated from ice slab refrigeration is used to heat the adjacent swimming pool, thereby helping to optimize energy performance by a projected 38 percent, or 490,000 equivalent kilowatt hours per year. In 2009, the project was recognised with an Excellence for Green Building Award from the Globe Foundation and World Green Building Council.

4

5

6

Site Plan:
1. New ice rink
2. New lobby
3. Existing pool
4. Existing community centre
5. Existing school

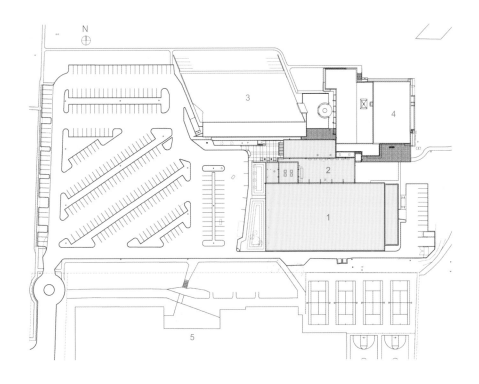

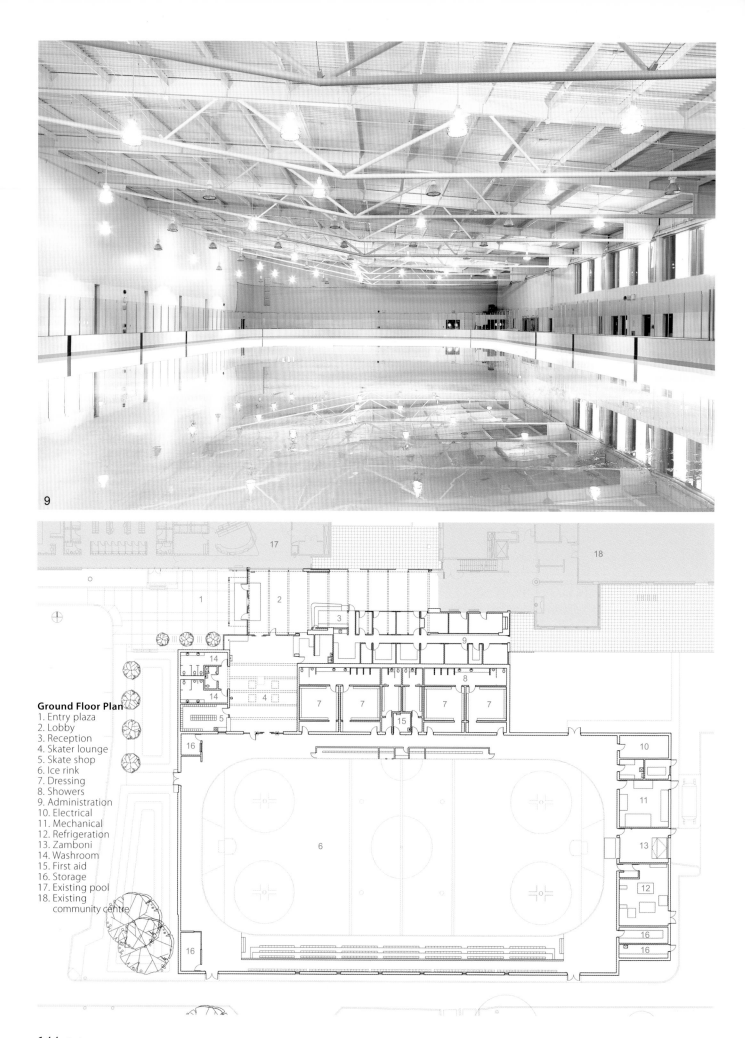

Ground Floor Plan
1. Entry plaza
2. Lobby
3. Reception
4. Skater lounge
5. Skate shop
6. Ice rink
7. Dressing
8. Showers
9. Administration
10. Electrical
11. Mechanical
12. Refrigeration
13. Zamboni
14. Washroom
15. First aid
16. Storage
17. Existing pool
18. Existing
    community centre

9,10. Ice rink

1

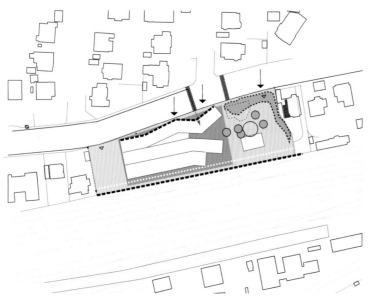

Site Plan/Surroundings

Community Centre, Gersonsvej

Architects:
Dorte Mandrup Arkitekter ApS
Location:
Gersonsvej, Denmark
Project area:
2,600m²
Project year:
2008
Photographs:
© Adam Mork

The building is situated in a residential area in the northern suburb of Copenhagen, Denmark. The area predominately consists of large villas from the turn of the century. The site is long and narrow – on one side bordering the railroad and on the other a busy road-Gersonsvej – hence there was a noise problem to be solved.

The programme was a mixed use complex containing several different institutions both communities and individual users. Cross programming was developed through workshops and games with future users, adults as well as children.

The site is noise polluted in a degree demanding noise reducing walls to protect the outdoor play area. Elements such as a bunker and a transformer box were integrated in the landscape of green noise baffles surrounding the site. An old chestnut tree — characteristic for the site — was preserved and incorporated in the garden.

To express the complexity of the programme under one roof, the building is shaped to the area with a form that morph recreation and leisure in three connected houses. As interpretations of the surrounding villas, the design of the building basically downscales the large volume of the gym to the scale of the area. There is a dynamic synergy between the villas and throughout the house, where sports and leisure are directly intertwined, both physically and mentally. The merge

2

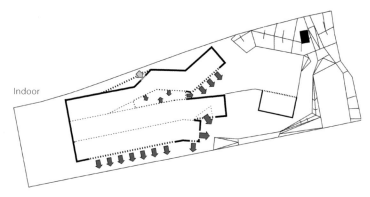

Indoor

1. Work shop & café
2. Enclosed court
3. Street elevation
4. North elevation

between indoors and outdoors was also in relation to this and an important feature for the users. Ground level activities all have direct access to the garden or court yards.

The terminology of the building recognizes classical domestic spaces such as the entrance hall, dining room, atelier, living room, terrace, garden and attic. Through the use of colour, light and surfaces, varying moods are emerging as a series of rooms. Each is done with its own special character, specific technical, acoustic, material and surface related qualities depending on their unique function.

The ambition has been to create a hangout for children, who recall Pippi Long Stockings, famous 'Villa Villakulla' more than just another institution.

1. Elevation
2. South elevation
3, 4. Cross section
5. Longitude section
6. Villas built together
7. Adjustment to surroundings

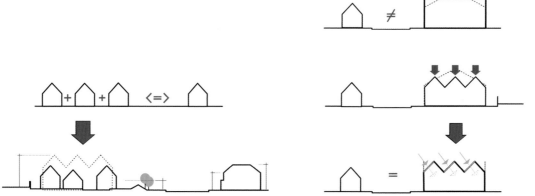

Ground Floor Plan:
1. Disposal
2. Multipurpose gym
3. Main entrance
4. Lounge
5. Dressing
6. Hall
7. Entry room
8. Motor coordination play room
9. Scullery
10. Heart of the building
11. Studio
12. Kitchen
13. Wood work shop
14. Dining room
15. Terrace
16. Waste
17. Garden
18. Enclosed court
19. Outdoor workshop

7. Heart of the building
8. Dressing

1

Lebenshilfe Weiz Centre

Architects:
EDERER + HAGHIRIAN
ARCHITEKTEN ZT-OG
Location: Weiz, Austria
Project area: 3,500m²
Project year: 2009
Photographs: © Paul Ott

The physical manifestation of this objective is the day centre, which was based at the Lebenshilfe's headquarters in Brachtergasse together with the full-time assisted living unit. Despite several additions, the capacity of these premises was exhausted, and so an invited architectural competition was held. The task was to build a new day centre on a nearby disused allotment site. The new centre was to serve as a place for people to come together at different levels.

In this first-prize-winning design, Ederer and Haghirian therefore apply the fundamental creed of 'self-confident integration' to the concept of their architecture, too.

The building site is located on a gentle slope on the eastern edge of the Weiz basin. A large settlement in the form of four-storey residential buildings, built in the 1960s, abuts on the site in the west. The rest of the site is surrounded by

2

1. Entrance
2. Terrace

older detached houses. One aim was to create a link between these two different scales. This was accomplished by the new building following the line of the street on two storeys on the side of the residential

blocks and thus forming a prestigious urban situation. On the slope side, the building is dug in so as to enter into a dialogue with the smaller neighbouring buildings in the form of a single-storey façade.

The new day centre is a clear-cut cubic body. By means of its strip windows and white plaster, it evokes memories of the elegant design of residential, health and leisure buildings of classical modernism. The façades are accentuated by incisions, whose wooden covering is somehow suggestive of a soft core of the volume.

The building is entered through a stately lobby, from where the lift and stairs go up to the upper storey. On the left, this area

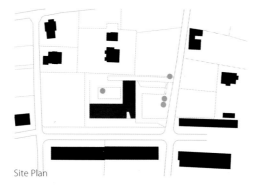

Site Plan

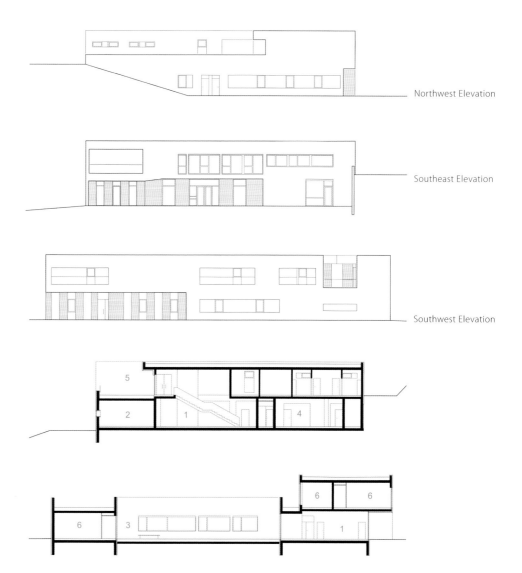

Northwest Elevation

Southeast Elevation

Southwest Elevation

Sections:
1. Lobby
2. Café
3. Courtyard
4. Kitchen
5. Terrace
6. Office

is flanked by the guest service area. This fully appointed café is a meeting-place for visitors to the centre and also serves as an exhibition space for the goods produced here. This is adjoined by a dining-room served by a self-operated, professionally equipped kitchen.

A central element of the design is the wood-covered interior courtyard with its tree. Arranged around it are the dining-room, therapy, work and group rooms for the fifty people working here. It serves as a multifunctional leisure area and as a 'landmark'. By means of the clever positioning of the surrounding rooms and the generous use of opaque and transparent glazing, the rooms and corridors all have natural lighting.

The building's ring-shaped circulation offers a circular walk rich in variety, that affords views both inside and outside the building. The actual work areas are divided into a textile, wood and open creative/art workshop. In order to emphasise the different workshops, the floors are of different colours. In general-use areas, an inconspicuous signage system helps people find their way around, with carpentered installations such as cloak-rooms and kitchens accentuated with special colours.

The top floor houses the administrative and staff rooms, along with the day centre — an area that provides care for young people and adults with high-level and highest-level disabilities. This facility benefits particularly from the

4

3. View from upper level into dining room and terrace
4. Dining room

many different opportunities offered by the building in terms of function and communication. Both the day centre and the staff area have spacious terraces for outdoor leisure and activities. The situation on the slope means that both storeys have barrier-free access, thus avoiding the need for complicated fire-protection measures that would detract from the open layout of the rooms.

In this way, the architects have created a spatial continuum that, like a 'promenade architecture', offers its occupants a host of different appeals and opportunities to experience the building with their senses. The sequence of concentrated work areas and clearly arranged communicative zones gives the people working here freedom of choice and ideal conditions for productive coexistence.

5

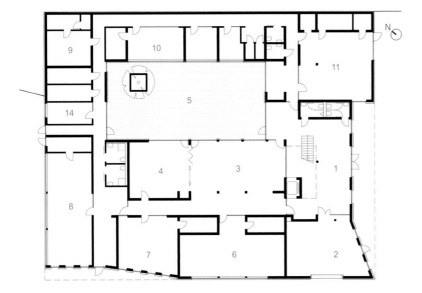

Ground Floor Plan (Left) and First Floor Plan (Facing Below):
1. Lobby
2. Café
3. Dining room
4. Therapy
5. Courtyard
6. Creative/Art workshop
7. Textil workshop
8. wood workshop
9. Technics
10. Attendance
11. Kitchen
12. Group room
13. Terrace
14. Office
15. Archive
16. Seminar room
17. Staff room

5. Group room
6. View into the courtyard

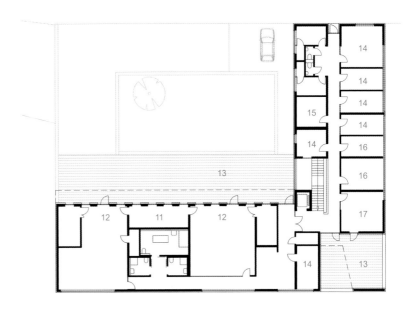

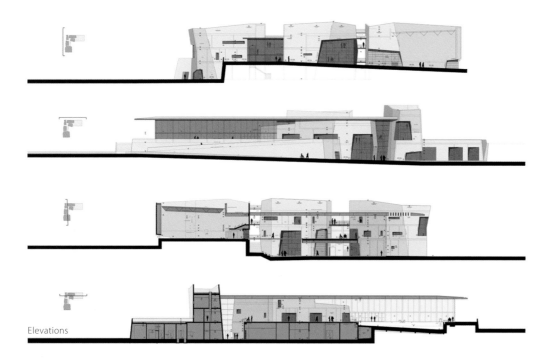

Elevations

Beit-Halochem

Architects:
Kimmel Eshkolot Architects
Location:
Be'er Sheva, Israel
Project area:
18,000m²
Project year:
2011
Photographs:
© Amit Giron
Award:
The Rechter Architecture Prize, 2011

On the outskirts of Beer Sheva, where the city ends and the desert begins, is the site of a new building: Beit Halochem (Veterans' Home).

The scorching desert sun and the parched scenery served as inspiration. The structure was designed as an arrangement of 'rock' like units grouped together. Between them a thin horizontal roof forms a courtyard – intimate, inviting and protected, to serve the functions of the building – a home for disabled veterans and their families.

While studying the various three-dimensional expanses, a unique relationship with the project emerged, based on relations between light and shadow, closed versus open, positive and negative. The bright sunlight makes it possible to achieve a three-dimensional richness by reflections from the rough frontal surfaces.

The 'rocks' enclose rooms for private and more intimate functions, while in-between spaces serve as public areas in the building. Light bridges spanned over those areas enable passage between public spaces, which reinforces the 'experience' of the building for the users.

In the private areas, thick walls provide climate protection, which is so essential in the Negev desert. In contrast, in the public areas the light roof that caps the building provides shade and protection of the interior regions, and also creates a variety

1. Façade
2. Entrance
3. Elevation
4. View of children's pool
5. Lobby
6. Hydrotherapeutic pool
7. Swimming pool

of external spaces where it is pleasant to relax.

The building divides the site into new topographies. This allowed the design of two ground floors on two different levels, interlocking with each other, as an integral part of the building architecture. Thus achieving maximum accessibility as is appropriate for the special needs of users of the building.

בית הלוחם
BET HALOCHEM

3

8. Sports hall

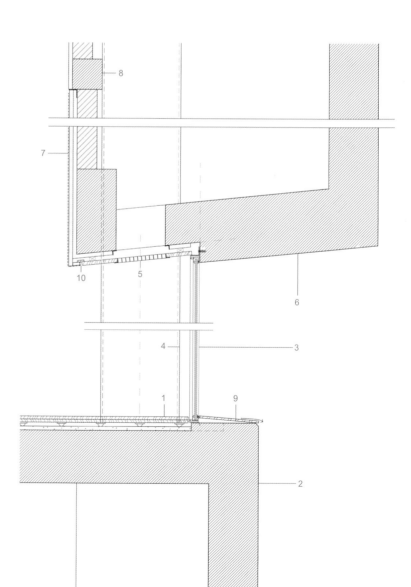

Bottom of Gym's Wall Detail:
1. Floating parquet floor
2. Concrete
3. Tempered glass window
4. 40" steel column
5. Wood panel with AC Hatch
6. Slanted concrete wall 10%
7. 20mm foam protecting panel
8. 25mm offset to align with protecting panel
9. Galvanized threshold+aluminium profile 10/10
10. Inner wood profile

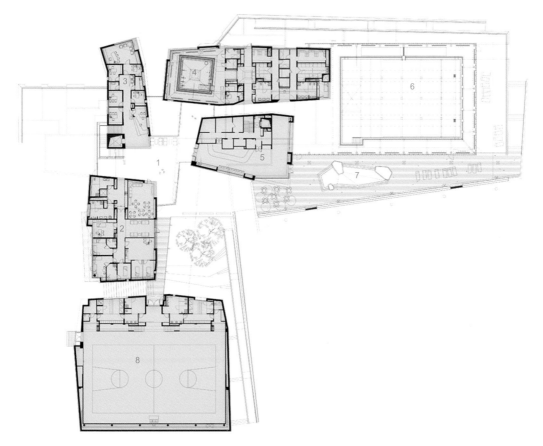

Floor Plan 1:
1. Main lobby
2. Physiotherapy
3. Administration
4. Hydrotherapeutic pool
5. Cafeteria
6. Swimming pool
7. Children's Pool
8. Sport hall

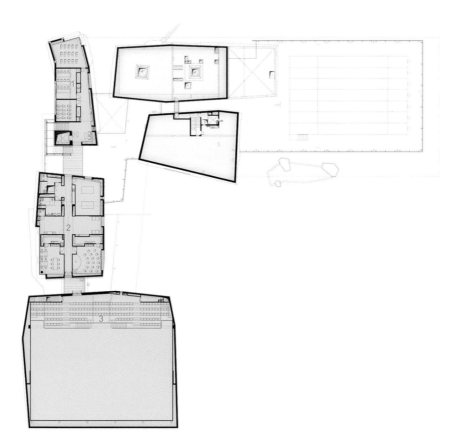

Floor Plan 2:
1. Multi-purpose classes
2. Art studios
3. Sport hall

Dalkeith Heights Community Building

Architects:
Adam Dettrick Architect Pty Ltd
Location:
Traralgon, VIC, Australia
Project year: 2010
Photographs:
© Michael Downes, UA Creative
Award:
Victorian Architecture Awards:
Regional Prize 2011

Dalkeith Heights is a new socially and ecologically sustainable lifestyle village in Traralgon, Victoria, Australia. The clients, Grace Bruce & JL MacMillan Memorial Home Inc. have a vision to create a state of the art new community that will set a new standard in lifestyle options for the Latrobe Valley region. The architects have been engaged to provide master planning, urban design and architecture that achieves their vision.

The $40 Million project includes over 150 houses, 18 assisted apartments, and a community building offering resort style amenities. Buildings are designed to be energy efficient, low carbon, and environmentally friendly.

The community building is the modern, welcoming heart of the new community. It is a multi-purpose building with many lifestyle and health features including bar, restaurant, café, cinema, gym, pool, doctor rooms, pharmacy and hairdresser. A warm, modern style has been created for the building, demonstrating that architecture for older citizens does not always have to feel old to be successful.

The building has been designed to create a sheltered north facing courtyard around a grand old redgum tree. As the village develops, lawn bowls, bocce and a village green will become extensions to the courtyard to complete the active, social hub of the new community.

1. Façade
2. South elevation
3. West elevation

The social and environmental aspirations of Dalkeith Heights are embedded in this new building. Socially, it is designed to be activated by its many functions all opening onto its central courtyard. Environmentally, it has been designed to minimise its environmental impact in design, construction and operation.

Timber framing has been employed to minimise structural steel in the building, and the design is tailored to the site to protect from sun and wind. High levels of insulation and thermal mass have been incorporated within the building to provide superior levels of energy efficiency, and lower operating costs.

In awarding the Regional Prize 2011, the Victorian Architecture Awards jury gave this citation: 'Offering a vibrant place for communal activity within a retirement village and catering for multiple levels of dependence, this building sets a new standard of architectural excellence for its type in the region.'

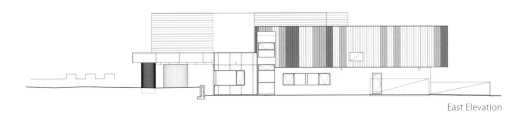

East Elevation

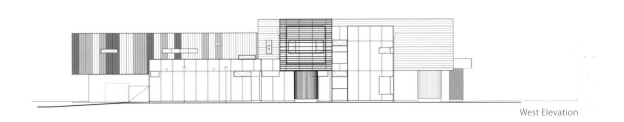

West Elevation

South Elevation

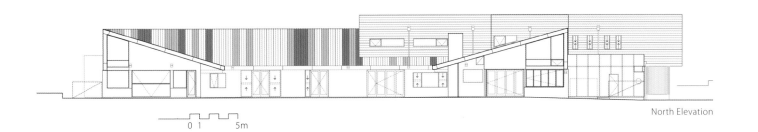

North Elevation

0 1   5m

173

4. North elevation
5. Entry
6. Bar
7. Restaurant
8. Library
9. Pool

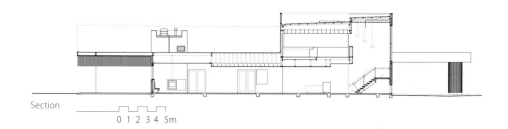

Section

0 1 2 3 4 5m

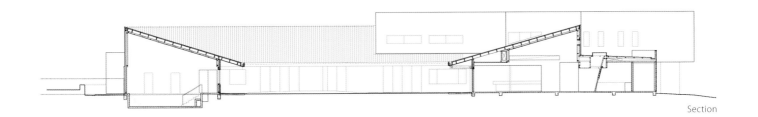

Section

9

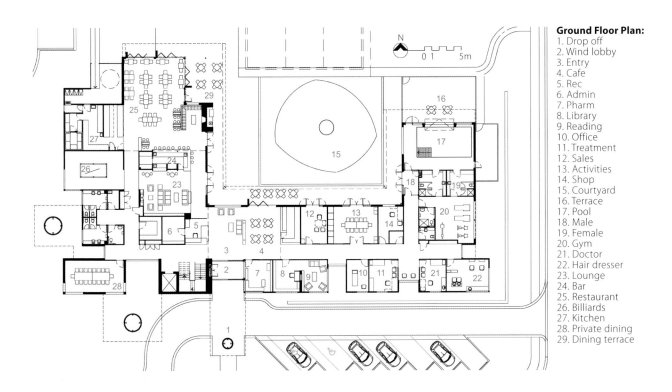

Ground Floor Plan:
1. Drop off
2. Wind lobby
3. Entry
4. Cafe
5. Rec
6. Admin
7. Pharm
8. Library
9. Reading
10. Office
11. Treatment
12. Sales
13. Activities
14. Shop
15. Courtyard
16. Terrace
17. Pool
18. Male
19. Female
20. Gym
21. Doctor
22. Hair dresser
23. Lounge
24. Bar
25. Restaurant
26. Billiards
27. Kitchen
28. Private dining
29. Dining terrace

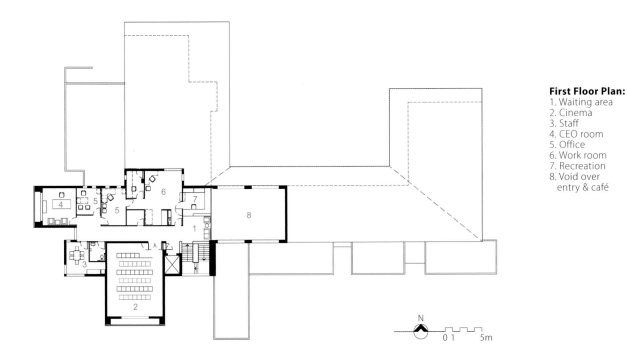

First Floor Plan:
1. Waiting area
2. Cinema
3. Staff
4. CEO room
5. Office
6. Work room
7. Recreation
8. Void over
   entry & café

1

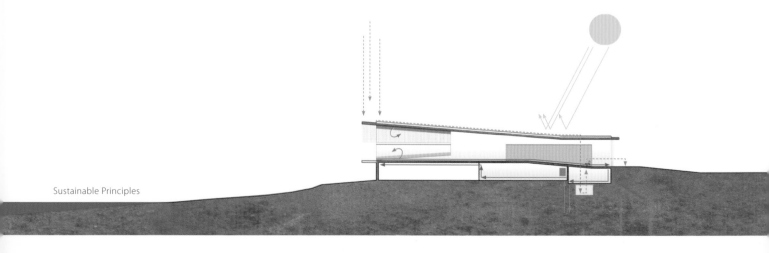

Sustainable Principles

Community Centre Pointe-Valaine

Architects:
Smith Vigeant architectes
Location:
Otterburn Park, Quebec, Canada
Construction area:
808m²
Project year:
2007
Photographs:
© Yves Beaulieu

As a social, cultural, and recreational centre, the Pointe-Valaine pavilion has become a healthy expression of community development. Situated on the Richelieu River, it is the fulcrum between earth and water. As the beach emerges from the river, the pavilion emerges from the community.

Initially the project revolved around the rebuilding of the once famous 'Club de canotage d'Otterburn Park', founded in 1921 that fell victim to flames a few years ago. Therefore, the project's approach began with an exploration of the site's history as a source for understanding the community's vernacular design.

The main floor includes an exhibition and meeting hall with a 200 seating capacity, a smaller 12 person meeting room as well as office and support spaces. Animated by the conscious insertion of natural lighting and ventilation, the exhibition hall operates as a gallery for local artists.

As with traditional canoe clubs, the large community hall is surrounded by a wooden veranda and opens on to the Richelieu River. It is the location of club meetings, municipal assemblies, and celebrations year round. At the lower level, the building houses storage space for canoes, kayaks and recreational material, a workshop, lockers and showers for the users. Easily accessible, the spaces are linked by a play of levels and ramps that encourages fluid indoor/outdoor connections.

1. Southwest elevation
2. Southeast elevation
3. Entrance
4. Lobby
5. Canoe/kayak storage

During the conception, environmental impacts were analyzed at several levels including the immediacy of personal comfort, the health of the community and the reduction of ecological footprint. Site Integration, building performance and water conservation and management were all important elements of the design strategy.

The project design favoured noble and recycled materials and the natural inherent finishes associated with them. The city of Otterburn Park was eager to support this sustainable project as a reflection of the community's values in order the help Pointe-Valaine reaffirm its vocation as an eco-recreational park.

Awards:

- PCI design awards 2010 'Recognized for design excellence, sustainability, and innovation'
- Green building sab awards & cagbc 2009, Sustainable architecture & building excellence in Canada
- Prix d'excellence de la construction en acier icca-cisc, Catégorie bâtiment verts 2008 – 'stratégie d'ensemble des mesures durables appliquées'
- Trophées innovation contech 2008, Dans la catégorie développement durable-pratiques novatrices

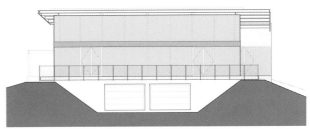

Southeast Elevation

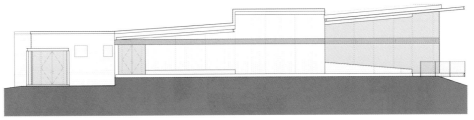

Northwest Elevation

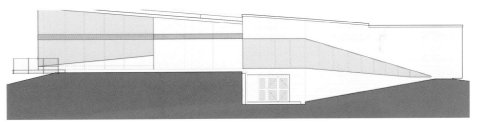

Southwest Elevation

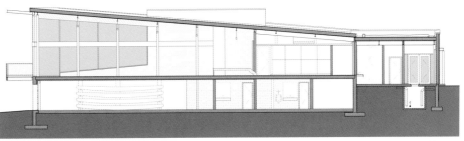

Section

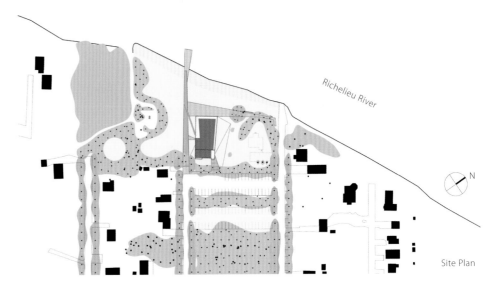

Richelieu River

N

Site Plan

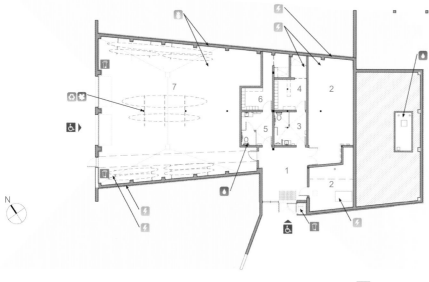

Basement Plan:
1. Entrance
2. Storage
3. Men's washroom
4. Men's changeroom
5. Women's washroom
6. Women's changeroom
7. Canoe/Kayak storage

N

	Recycling		Universal Accesability
	Natural Finishes		Material Recuperation
	Passif Solar Energy		Water Consumption
	Energie Consumtion		Prefabrication
			Local Materials

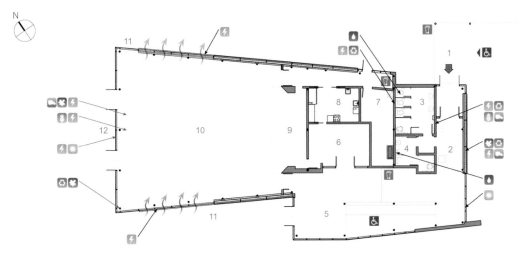

Main Floor Plan:
1. Entrance
2. Entry hall
3. Women's washroom
4. Men's washroom
5. Exhibition hall
6. Conference room
7. Storage
8. Kitchen
9. Snackbar
10. Community hall
11. Ramp
12. Veranda

1

The Culture Yard

Architects:
AART architects
Location:
Elsinore, Denmark
Project area:
17,000m²
Project year:
2010
Photographs:
© Adam Mørk

In many years the attention has been aimed at the site adjacent, where the UNESCO World Heritage site, Kronborg Castle, which is famous for its role in Shakespeare's Hamlet, exerts its magnetic pull on both tourists and local citizens of Elsinore – but now Elsinore's old shipbuilding yard has been transformed into a 17,000 m² cultural and knowledge centre, including concert halls, showrooms, conference rooms, a dockyard museum and a public library.

The Culture Yard symbolises Elsinore's transformation from an old industrial town to a modern cultural hub. In this way, the yard is designed as a hinge between the past and present, reinforcing the identity of the local community, but at the same time expressing an international attitude,

reinforcing the relation between the local and global community.

The contrast between past and present permeates the Culture Yard. For instance, the original concrete skeleton with armoured steel has been reinforced, but left exposed as a reference to the area's industrial past. The historic context has thus been the main structural idea in the design process, ensuring the keen observer will discover a chapter of history in every corner of the yard and every peeling of the wall. In other words, if you want to understand what Elsinore really is, what the intangible blur between past and present feels like, this is the place to visit. Thanks to architectural features such as wrought iron stairs and concrete elements,

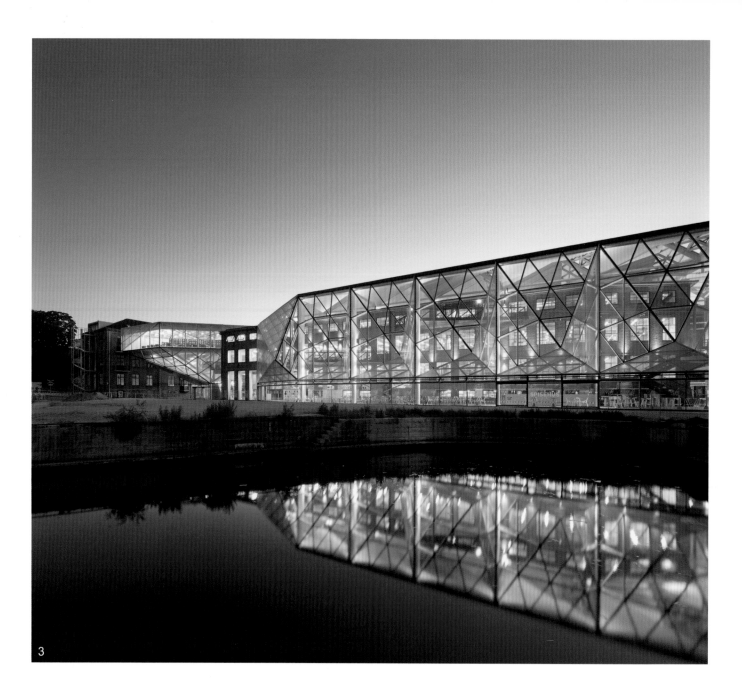

3

interacting with modern glass structures and interior designs, the contrast between the days of yore and the present becomes evident. It is the Culture Yard's way of playing with the field of tension between old and new, making the notion of past versus present, the industrial society versus the information society, constantly present.

Particularly striking, when viewed from the seafront and Kronborg Castle, is the multifaceted façade. Like a fragmented, yet strongly coherent structure, the enormous glass and steel façade challenges the historic site and stares unflinchingly across the Sound — the strait that separates Denmark and Sweden. The transparent façade also reinforces the relation between inside and outside, as you can peak in from

street level and enjoy the magnificent sea view and view of Kronborg Castle from every floor of the building, especially from the glass cave which in a dramatic gesture protrudes out of the building above the main entrance.

In this way, the façade encloses the yard in a distinctive atmosphere, as the dazzling and dramatic play of lines generates a sense of spaciousness. Although the façade is made of hundreds of lines and triangles it appears as one big volume, generating a sense of place and time. The volume also takes the environment into account, since the façade not only functions as an aesthetic and spatial architectural feature, but also as a climate shield, reducing the energy demand for cooling and heating of the building.

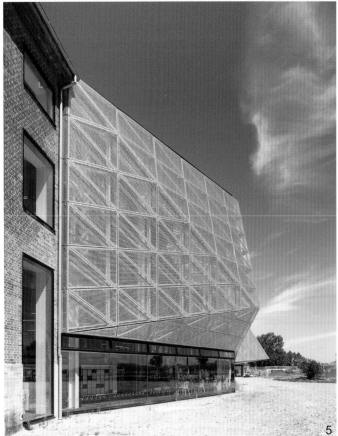

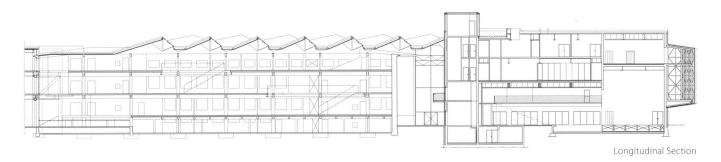

Longitudinal Section

4. The backyard has been preserved in order to reflect the site's industrial history.
5. The façade is designed as a climate shield, reducing the energy demand for cooling and heating of the building.

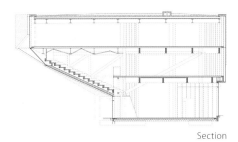

Section

6. Towards the city a metallic box radiates out from the original brick structure.
7. The stairs to the toilettes in the basement is designed as an exciting architectural feature.
8. The contrast between the past and present permeates the interior.

8

9

9. The arcade creates a varied inflow of daylight during the day.
10. Even the floors reflect the Culture Yard's industrial past.
11-12. From 'the Horizon' the visitors can enjoy the magnificent view towards the sea and Kronborg Castle.

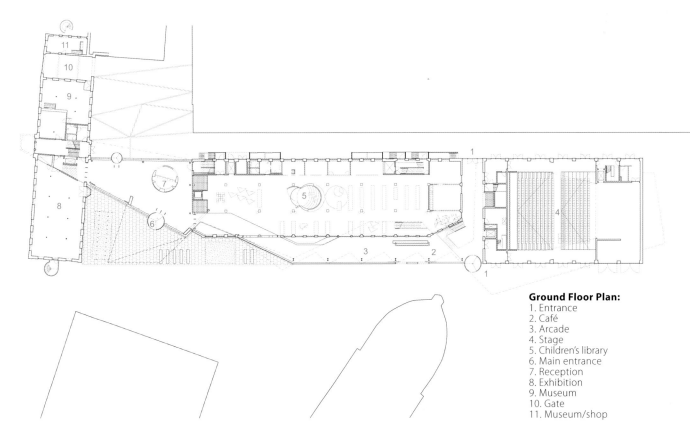

Ground Floor Plan:
1. Entrance
2. Café
3. Arcade
4. Stage
5. Children's library
6. Main entrance
7. Reception
8. Exhibition
9. Museum
10. Gate
11. Museum/shop

13. The foyer creates a casual and accommodating arrival to the Culture Yard.
14. The Culture Yard includes two concert halls.
15. The public library is the main function of the Culture Yard.
16. The public library provides a perfect setting for children.
17. The public library has a wide range of niches for relaxation, reading or talking.

Temple Sinai Community Centre

Architects:
Michael Harris and Mark Horton
Location:
Oakland, California, USA
Project area:
1,746.5m²
Project year:
2010
Photographs:
© Ethan Kaplan Photography

Temple Sinai is very much a part of the larger community around it, and to that end they wanted openness where views into the buildings and out to the City of Oakland were maintained. This sense of community goes further with the Jewish concept of tikkun olam, 'repairing the world,' and to this end LEED certification was an important goal.

The community centre has grown around their 1918 landmarked sanctuary with new buildings in a way that has disassociated all of their different activities for the

nearby residence. The Temple's new building programme included classrooms, a preschool, administrative offices, and a library, but most importantly the temple wanted a new design to organise these disparate elements into a place where their congregants could feel a greater sense of community where people could meet each other in casual spaces for spontaneous conversation.

A circulation spine, which runs the length of the building and joins all programmatic elements, has a wall of mosaic stone tile

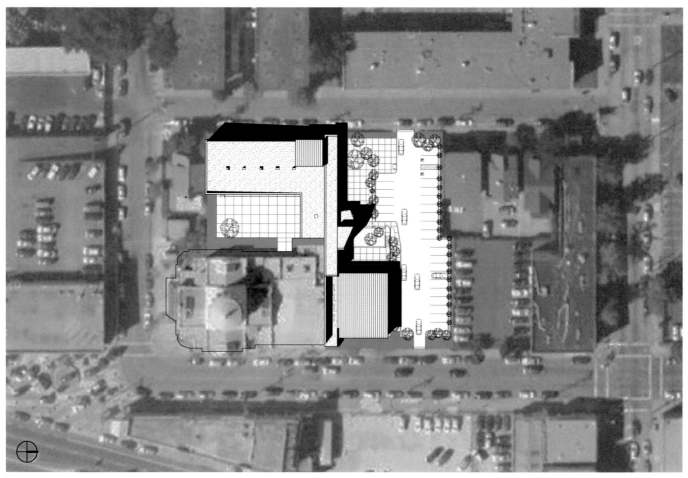

Site Plan

of the same length and material as one of Judaism's most sacred sites, the Western Wall in Jerusalem. This is the space where all parts of the temple community meet and to which are attached three jewel-like building objects wrapped in green-tinted zinc cladding: the chapel, the community living room, and the library.

Other architectural details and spaces draw heavily on Jewish history and tradition as well; the chapel inspired by the tallit, or prayer shawl, enfolds worshippers in wood slat walls and ceiling (forming a continuous band) recalling the wooden shuls, the pre-war synagogues of eastern Europe. By day one can look through the text of the v'ahafta, a prayer central to Jewish practice, on the high band of windows to see sky; by night the prayer's white letters stand out against the dark. Along the stone mosaic wall are weathered copper plaques with quotes from Jewish scholars and poets.

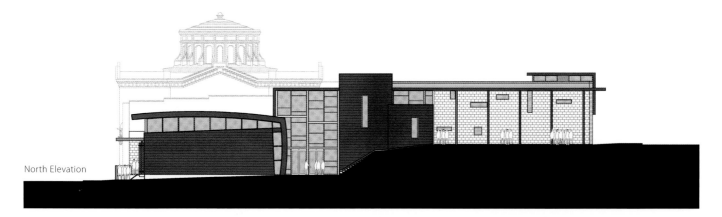

North Elevation

1. Entrance
2. North elevation

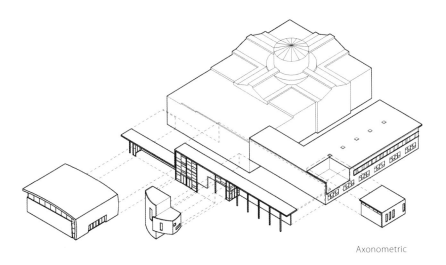

Axonometric

3. North elevation
4. Detail
5. Stairs
6. Play yard

6

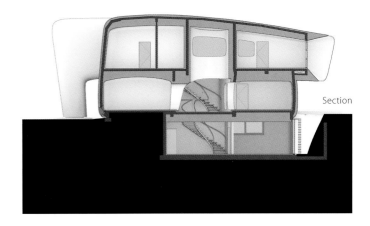

Section

7

7. Classroom
8. Interior detail

Floor Plan:
1. Entry colonnade
2. Library
3. Classrooms
4. Living room
5. Chapel
6. Existing sanctuary
7. Existing social hall
8. Entry foyer
9. Sacred outdoor space
10. Play yard

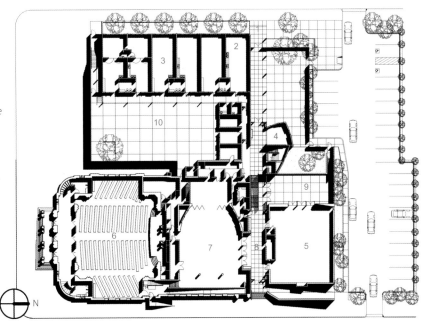

1

2

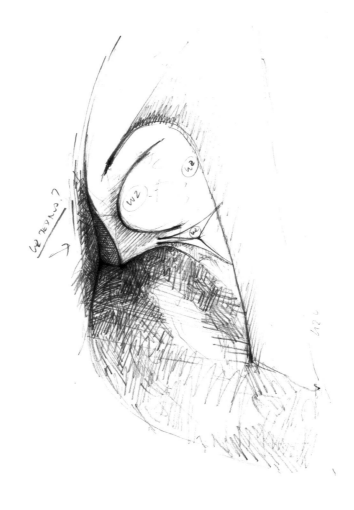

Community Centre
Senhora da Boa Nova

Architects:
Francisco Vaz Monteiro
and Filipa Roseta
Location:
Estoril, Portugal
Project area: 3,940.78m²
Project year: 2010
Photographs:
© Joao Morgado

The site's name was the 'End of the World'. It was one of the city's last slums. The project brief was determined through a participative process involving everyone in the local community in order to guarantee the project's social and economical sustainability. The final brief included a church, a community centre (providing jobs and childcare to some of the slum's former residents), a primary school and an auditorium.

The local community set as one of the main goals the creation a new identity in order to rescue the site from its decade long negative stigma. To the East and South, anonymous suburban surroundings offered no interesting references; hence, the architects decided to design the church's tower as an iconic reference.

To the West, the architects designed a courtyard connecting to the city's existing public spaces and opening to a steep valley offering distant seaside views. Today, the 'End of the World' is known as Senhora da Boa Nova (or Our Lady of the 'Good News').

The architects believe designing sacred space should revolve around the ability

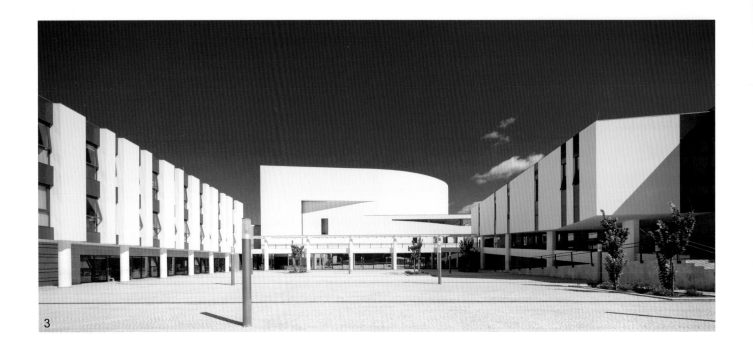

1. Church/Auditorium
2. Landscape
3. Main view
4-5. Entrance of Community Centre

to state the supremacy of the Void. Throughout the project's development, the key conceptual elements were two empty spaces: the courtyard, a place where the community could meet; and the nave, a sacred space presenting that which could not be presented. They wished the nave to be an introspective, infinite, and irrepresentable space. In order to achieve this, the architects followed creative paths suggested by the works of Bernini, Piranesi and Rachel Whiteread.

Today, the church stands within an elliptical plan, providing a dynamic sense of scale, and covered by an interior dome, eliminating the wall/ceiling division and spatial references within. The windows are deep, bringing indirect natural lighting into the nave and distancing the suburban surroundings, and the exterior walls curve to present an anthropomorphic object holding within the unlimited, infinite, and irrepresentable Void.

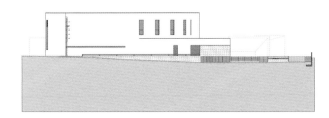
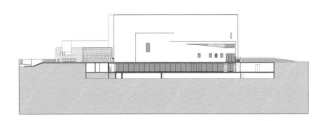

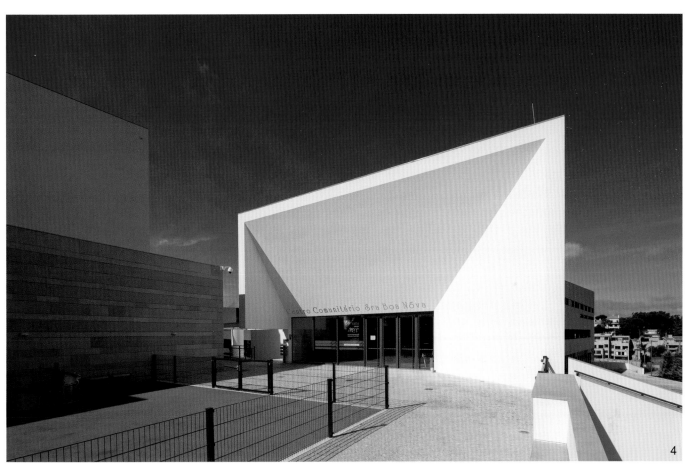

6-7. Church/Auditorium

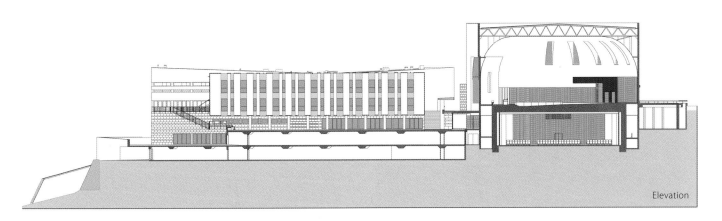

Elevation

8

Site Plan:
A. Church/Aluditorium (lower level)
B. Community Centre
C. Primary School
D. Courtyard (parking underground levels)

N

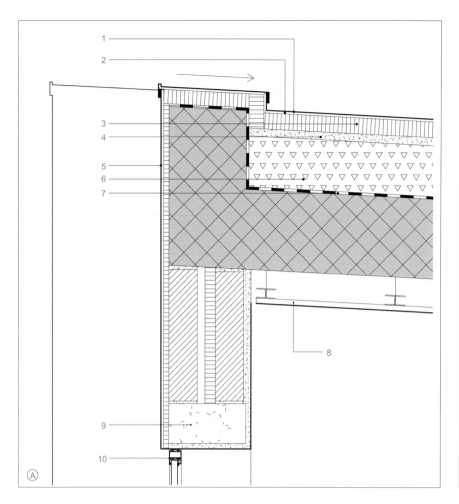

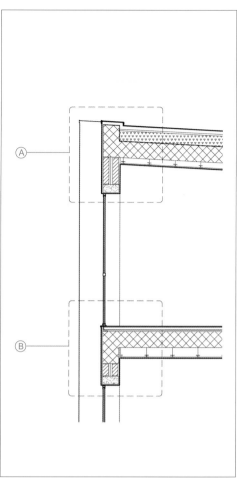

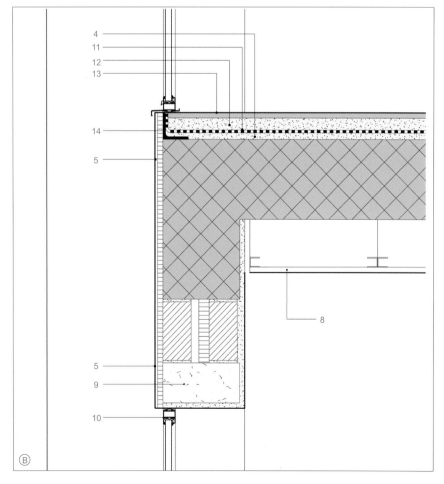

Façade Section 1:
1. Zinc standing seam covering
2. High density polyethylen membrane
3. Thermic insulation
4. Cement screed
5. Aluminium sheet
6. Light concrete
7. Waterproofing
8. Suspended plasterboard
9. Precast concrete lintel
10. Aluminium window frame
11. Acoustic insulation
12. Reinforced concrete slab
13. Epoxy-resin coating
14. Steel beam LPN 30

Façade Section 2:
1. Aluminium sheet
2. Precast concrete lintel
3. Aluminium window frame
4. Tiled blue Ataíja stone
5. Dry wall painted white
6. Oak paneling

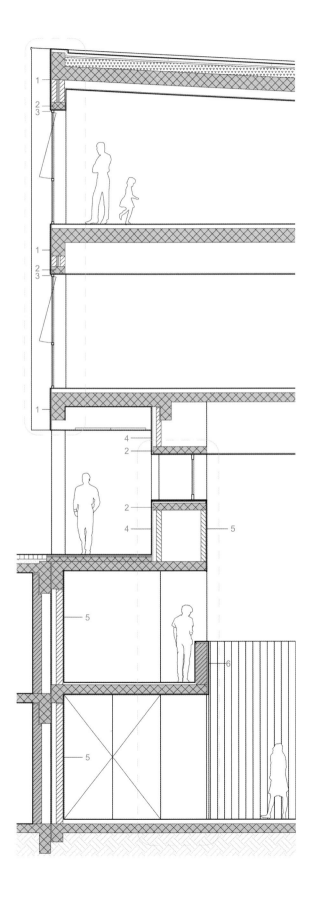

9. Facade
10. Sports Hall

Elevation

Section

Maison du Chemin de l'Île Community House

Architects:
archi5
Location:
Nanterre, France
Project area: 1,246m²
Project year: 2009
Photographs:
© Courtesy of archi5

This Community House is a project divided in three purposes: childhood activities centre, multi-use hall and a senior activities home.

Located in a heterogeneous neighbourhood with big social housings all around, this project, by assembling small spaces and presenting a small size, develops the theme of scale game. The first scale is the expression of a public building, open to every people. The second scale is more intimate, like a welcoming house where each purpose is defined by specific spaces with proper identities.

The mineral frontage on the Boulevard is set on a pedestal slightly above, down the street line, letting the place for a lavender field and a walking and meeting space. This free space informs about the public specific character front of the edifice.

1. General east view
2. South aerial view
3. Close east view
4. South view

By opposition to the regularity of the 'city side' of the project, the inside spaces are open to the intimacy of the gardens located into the building body. Sheltered by a wide sloping copper roof, the composition reflects the playful character of the early childhood house.

Two central courtyards, planted with olive trees, ensure the unity of the project. It provides shaded meeting or restoring spaces for the multiple users. On the other side of the building, the curvy Douglas Pine façade gives to the playfield a character of intimacy and welfare, just like in a house garden.

This house is a High Environmental Quality project. The architects tried, from the conception to the realisation, to minimise nuisance, waste and pollution. They also decided to include a maximum of ecological and economic devices to make energy economy and reduce the ecological print of this house: Wood boiler, Canadian wells, Double-flow ventilation, Light Douglas Pine façades highly isolated, Local oak interior woodwork, Vegetated roof and Conservation of existing trees.

From the beginning of the project, this community house is conceived like a place where youth people can meet third age people, where every people of community could feel this place like a public home open to everybody. This 'maison' acts as a melting pot at the neighbourhood level.

3

4

217

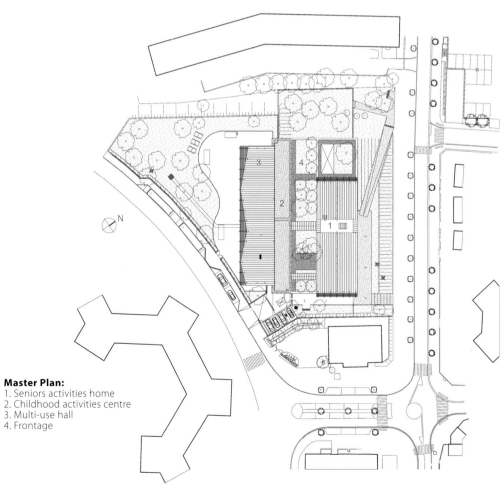

Master Plan:
1. Seniors activities home
2. Childhood activities centre
3. Multi-use hall
4. Frontage

5. North corner
6. Senior activities hall

7

7-8. Children activities hall

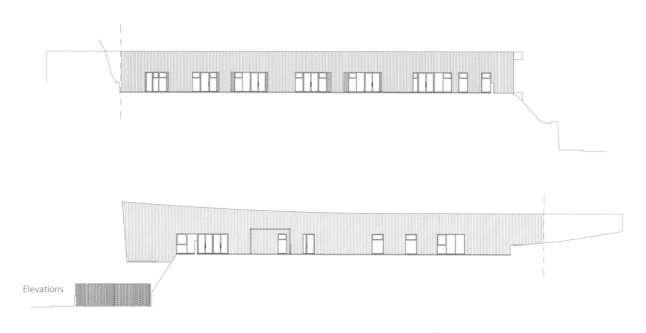

Elevations

Centre of Social Services in Montealto

Architects:
Naos Architecture (Santiago González & Mónica Fernández, Architects)
Location: A Coruña, Spain
Site area: 5,239.7m²
Construction area: 3,264.8m²
Project year: 2010
Photographs:
© Naos Architecture, Amador Lorenzo

The Centre of Social Services in Montealto (A Coruña, Spain) is located in the district of A Coruña, with large and growing population.

The plot has trapezoidal covering an area of 5.239,7 square metres. The building of a single floor houses different areas of use of this district. The functional programme is developed on the ground floor, which suggests an immediate understanding of the building. This is because is necessary to separate the different social uses and their typologies.

The Centre of Social Services is built in an elongated U shape, in the centre of which are common outdoors areas, with a uniformity façade enclosing the building. Here, the central space opens up accesses for vehicles as for pedestrians. There is a nearby courtyard, so that older people can also walk on a soft pavement without risk of falling.

The building was designed on efficient and clear way concerning circulations, accesses and organisation of the spaces. The project organised the social services in three different volumes but integrated by a common façade. Each space has specific functions according to needs of use. The area oriented to the east is part of children's space. A courtyard

3

1. This Centre is built in an elongated U-shape, in the centres of which are common outdoor areas, with a uniformity façade enclosing the building.
2. Access to the plot takes place on two points. It could be by a circulation ramp and for pedestrian accesses is possible to use an external lift, due to the different heights.
3. There is a visual continuity between both parts of the building.
4. In the Elder Day Centre, the roof rises to the top of the dining room so that in this point is possible to have privileged views.
5. The project organised the social services in three different volumes but integrated by a common façade.

and school gardens run parallel to the school, so there are direct accesses from the classrooms to the outside by large windows that provide natural light. Also a large covered courtyard has been designed for use in rainy days. The building of elder day centre is developed along the west side where the outer space with a terrace area is located and from it people have direct access to the dining room. The last volume of Centre of Social Services is in the south of the plot. This volume houses the service area and equipment room of the whole space.

There is a visual continuity between all parts of the building, from which there are views towards the sea. The far ends of the construction have been designed with large windows on both sides. The roof rises to the top of the dining room so that in this point is possible to have privileged views.

Access to the plot could be by a circulation ramp and for pedestrian accesses is possible to use an external lift, due to

the different heights. The big variations of the plot are resolved by green spaces around the building.

4

5

6. A courtyard and school gardens run parallel to the school, so there are direct accesses from the classrooms to the outside by large windows that provide natural light.

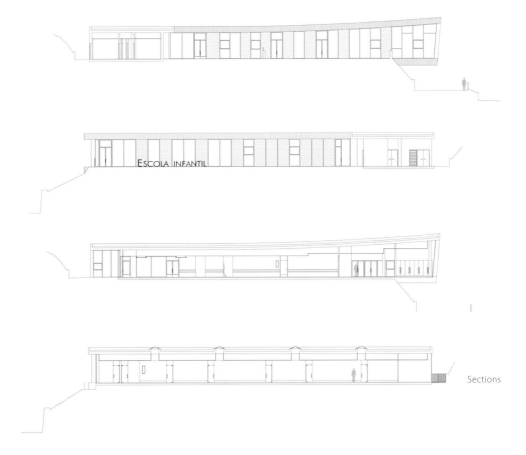

Sections

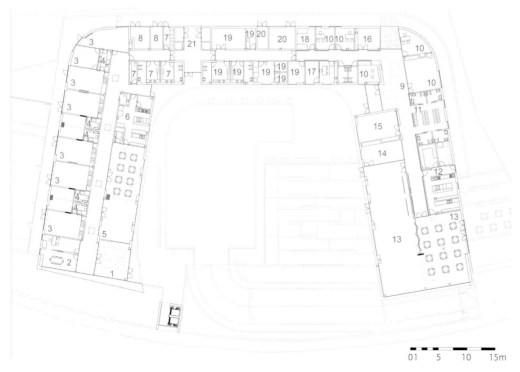

Ground Floor Plan:
1. Entrance hall
2. Teachers area
3. Classrooms
4. Toilets
5. Multi-purpose room/dining room
6. Kitchen
7. Auxiliary services room
8. Plants room
9. Entrance hall
10. Office of administration
11. Assisted toilets
12. Kitchen
13. Multi-purpose room/dining room
14. Occupational therapy room
15. Rehabilitation room
16. Treatment room
17. Specialized care room
18. Rest room
19. Auxiliary services room
20. Plants room
21. Maintenance area

01 5 10 15m

7-8. The functional programme is developed on the ground floor,
    with different social uses.
9-10. The building of a single floor houses two different areas of use:
    a Nursery School and an Elder Day Centre Both can enjoy the space between them.

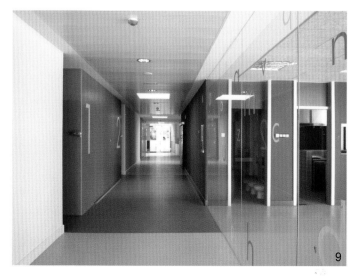

2

Moonee Valley Community Centre

Architects:
H2O Architects Pty Ltd.
Location:
Melbourne, Australia
Project area:
1,625m²
Project year:
2010
Photographs:
© Trevor Mein

Form (Twin Volumes + Covered Way):
Twin conjoined volumes – one high for the taller and much larger Library space and the other low mostly containing cellular rooms plus foyer – define the form. The new building is surrounded by adjacent car parking and landscaping and linked to an upgraded existing gymnasium.

**Special Qualities
(Change of Brief during Construction):**
The specific building type – LIBRARY evolved in an unusual manner. The facility was originally briefed as a Community Centre with two principal components – a 200 seat flat floor Multipurpose Hall for hire by local community groups and associated staff areas, foyer, amenities and flexible, wireless classrooms.

Mid way through construction the brief changed to a Community Library. The high ceilinged south lit MPR simply adapted into reading and reference area, support spaces generally maintained the same functions and one classroom was converted to Computer Lab.

**Originality
(Middle Eastern References):**
Deliberate choices were made of brightly coloured Trespa panelling as the primary cladding and the feature end wall palette of ceramic tile, timber, powder coat steel, alucobond and fritted glass to reflect the material choices and vivid colouring of the largely Middle Eastern users.

3

Innovation
(Quoting of Humphries and Arkley):
Materials and colours were chosen from examples amongst the local building stock. The building's innovative iconography reinterprets the lurid colourings and exaggerated realities of well known Australian artists, Barry Humphries and Howard Arkley in their depictions of the 'Oz' suburb.

Sustainability
(Low Energy):
The building was conceived as being low energy, naturally ventilated, heated and cooled, thermally efficient and utilising appropriate materials with low or no off-gassing. The saw tooth roof form allows maximum South light with no sun penetration into the Library.

Contexturalism
(Eclectic Ethnically Diverse Neighbourhood):
The design reflects its eclectic neighbourhood and attempts to recall a typical Anglo Saxon imagery for its mostly immigrant local residents.

1-2. South elevation
3. Landscape
4. Wall detail

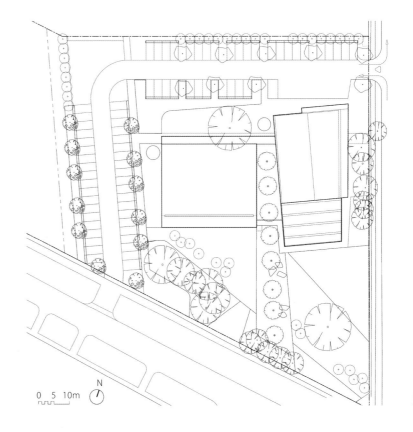

0 5 10m

N

4

5. Training room

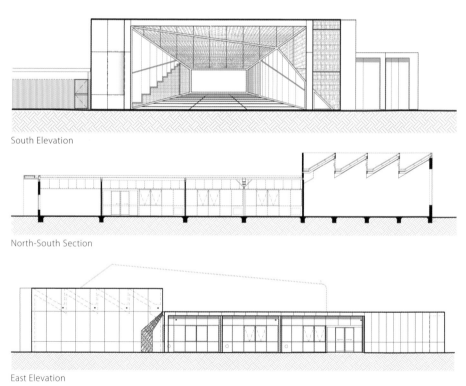

South Elevation

North-South Section

East Elevation

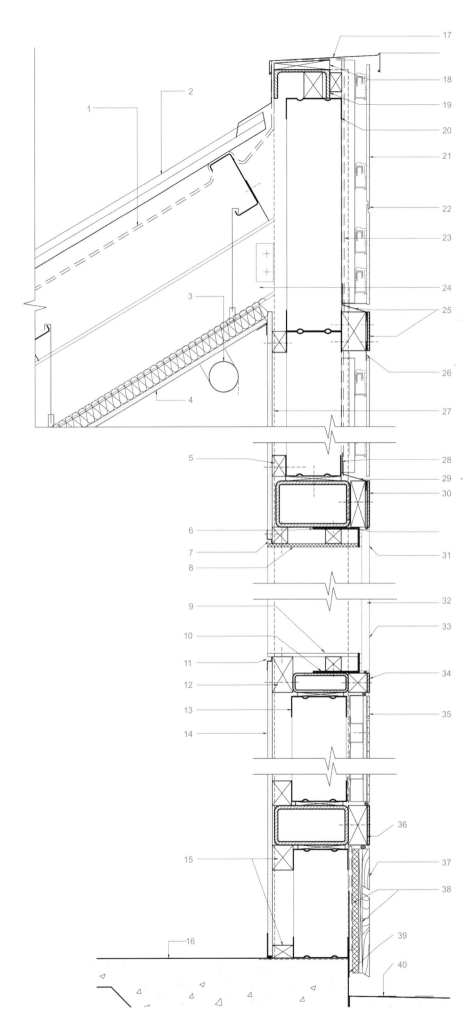

Detail:
1. R3.7 roof insulation
2. Kilp-lok 700series zincalume roof sheeting
3. Motorised blinds
4. On rondo screw-up suspended ceiling
   system finish with corner beads
5. Treated timber packer to suit
6. 125×50mm aluminilum angle
7. 10mm shadowline
8. 9mm W.R. plywood head&jamb paint finish
9. 9mm W.R. plywood sill&jamb paint finish
10. 125×50 anodised aluminium angle
11. 10mm shadowline
12. Treated timber packer to suit
13. 150mm steel stud
14. 13mm plasterboard
15. Treated timber packer to suit
16. 100mm thick concrete slab
17. Capping
18. Treated timber packer
19. RB8/150PFC REF. to engineers DWGS
20. 150mm steel stud
21. Trespa meteon façade cladding invisible
    fixing with inserts and screws
22. Halved joint
23. Sarking+air-cell permishield 65
24. 180UR18
25. Zincalume flashing sealed
    on metal plate+vermin mesh
26. Vermin mesh sealed on metal plate
27. C1 beyond
28. 150mm steel stud
29. Zincalume flashing sealed on metal plate
30. 6mm mild steel galvanized plate screw
    fixed on timber packer paint finish
31. 16.76mm laminated class on
    double sided tape&structural
    silicone to be verified by the glazing eng.
32. Structural silicone at vertical joints
33. 16.76 laminated glass on double
    sided tape&structural silicone
34. 150×50×6mm RHS with
    6mm mid steel galvanized plate
35. 100×100mm ceramic coloured tiles on 9mm
    compressed cement sheeting 2mm grout joint
36. 6mm mild steel galvanized plat. countersun
    screw fixed on timber packer paint finish
37. Timber cladding 19mm hardwood precoated
38. Continues sarking on the outside
    of studs+air cell permishield 65
39. Flashing behind plywood continuously
    sealed to edge of slab,150mm min upstand
40. New concrete path. rake to fall away from
    building ref landscaoe DWGS for details

233

6-8. Library stacks and reading area
9. Public Internet

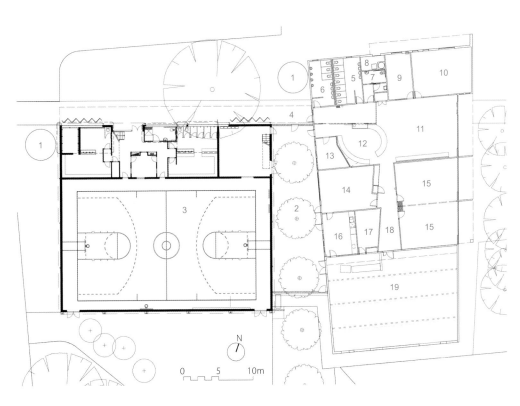

Floor Plan:
1. Water tank
2. Courtyard
3. Gymnasium
4. Entry
5. Female toilet
6. Male toilet
7. Disabled toilet
8. Plant room
9. Meeting room
10. Public internet
11. Reading area/
    Lounge area
12. Reception
13. Office
14. Staff workroom
15. Training room
16. Kitchen/
    Lunch room
17. Storeroom
18. Corridor
19. Library stacks
    and reading area

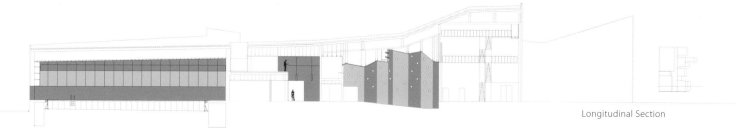

Longitudinal Section

Ibaiondo Civic Centre

Architects:
Jesús Armendáriz Eguillor, Amaia
Los Arcos Larumbe, David Resano
Resano/ACXT Architects
Location: Vitoria-Gasteiz, Spain
Project area: 14,000m²
Project year: 2009
Photographs: © Josema Cutillas

Ibaiondo Community Centre has a 14,000 sqm area and is located in Vitoria-Gasteiz (Spain). Sport, leisure and administrative services for neighbours at different parts of the city are joined together in these types of public buildings.

Once all interior functional, spatial and organizational requirements were defined, the project searched for an extroverted look to appeal the citizens, as to get the perception of the whole building to provide enough information of the public services to be provided there:

theatre, leisure and sports swimming pool, solarium, café, indoor sports centre, library, workshops, council citizens help points, etc.

The project avoids forms of an elaborate façade composition, and shows itself as irregular and polyhydric, with a leisure personality. Because of such diversity at interior layouts, the exterior catches the citizen's eye, specially the polymer concrete facades, with a multidirectional groove to create an optical polychromatic illusion.

2

The building interior layout follows extensive and strict functionality criteria defined by the Council technical team at competition phase. Sport services (swimming pool and indoor sports centre) are located to the north following a 'cartesian' geometry, due to their size and scale. So the rest of services are created to the south, with some sort of volumetric anarchy facing the residential area. Other uses are organized along a corridor separating and linking together different services. From this corridor, through glass enclosures, the visitor can recognise the different activities inside the building, as a suggestive 'showroom'.

Energy sustainability in the building is ratified by a high energy efficiency qualification, obtained by ensuring good thermal isolation and high equipment performances. Also an approximate 700 sqm area of solar thermal collectors provide energy to heat water for both swimming pool and building hot running water. This dedicated design generates an estimated CO_2 emissions saving of up to 1,900 Ton.

Detail:
1. Cavity-wall facade of concrete polymer panels 14mm
   -Aluminium profile 110mm
2. Polyurethane insulation 50mm
3. Concrete prefabricated panel 120mm
4. Glazed aluminium curtain wall
5. Double glass with low-E 70. 4+4.16.6
6. Roof decking system 150mm:
   -Galvanized Steel ribbed panel
   -Rockwool Panel insulation 80mm
   -PVC laminate 3 mm.
7. Reinforced concrete bases
8. Fill of graded crushed aggregate
9. Mortar cement
10. Mass slab floor
11. Crushed rock
12. Polyethylene waterproof laminate
13. Flashing steel galvanized 1mm
14. Prefabricated concrete beam20x60mm.
15. Prefabricated concrete Tie-beam 300mm.
16. Prefabricated concrete slab 300+50mm.
17. Concrete base with steel fibers reinforced 15cm
18. Prefabricated T concrete beam
19. Concrete brick wall 15cm width
20. Industrial epoxy resin, over smoothed concrete base 5mm
21. False ceiling gypsum board
22. Concrete strip footing

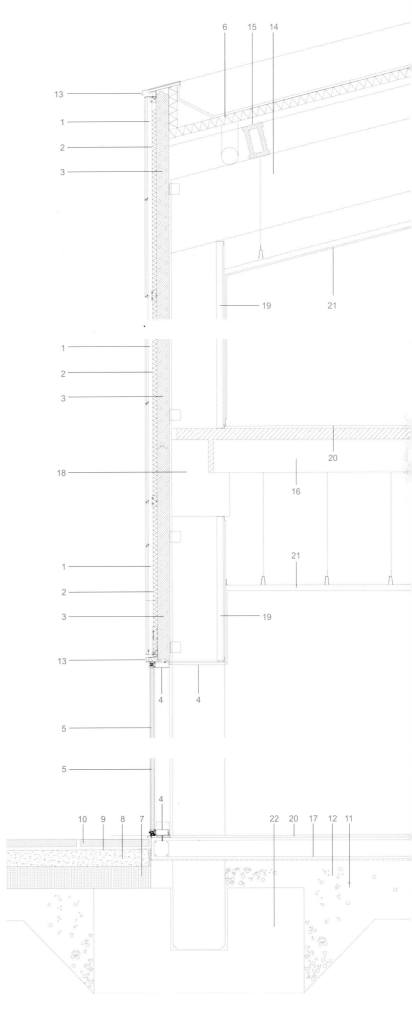

4-5. Corridor
6. Toy library access
7. Theatre

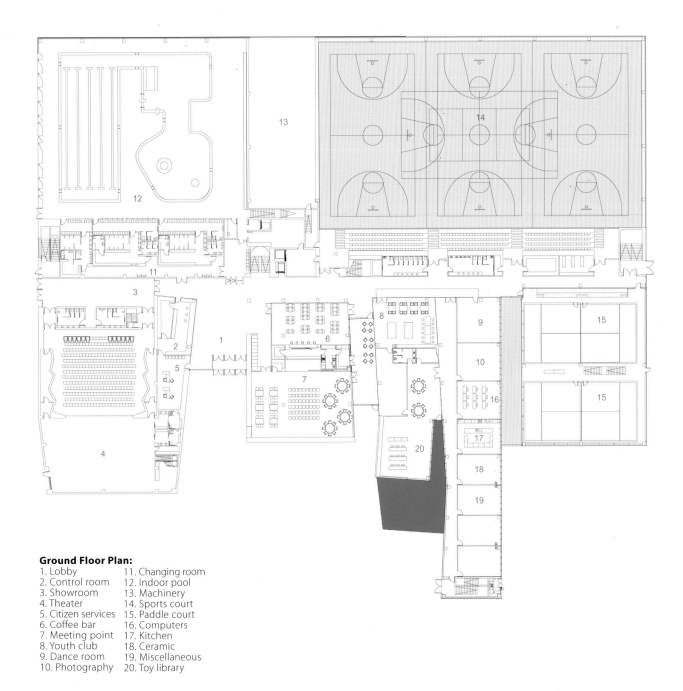

Ground Floor Plan:

1. Lobby
2. Control room
3. Showroom
4. Theater
5. Citizen services
6. Coffee bar
7. Meeting point
8. Youth club
9. Dance room
10. Photography
11. Changing room
12. Indoor pool
13. Machinery
14. Sports court
15. Paddle court
16. Computers
17. Kitchen
18. Ceramic
19. Miscellaneous
20. Toy library

INDEX

HCMA
hcma.ca
Suite 300,
1508 West 2nd Ave
Vancouver BC, Canada V6J 1H2
Tel: 604 732 6620
E-mail: office@hcma.ca

AART architects
aart.dk
Aaboulevarden 22, 5th floor
DK-8000 Aarhus C
Tel: +45 87 30 32 86
E-mail: aart@aart.dk

Johan De Wachter Architecten
www.jdwa.nl
Schiekade 189, 3013 BR,
Rotterdam
Tel: +31 102807032
E-mail: office@dwa.nl

Kimmel Eshkolot Architects
www.kimmel.co.il
27 Chelouche St. Tel Aviv 65149,
ISRAEL
Tel: 972-3-5176059
E-mail: manor@kimel.co.il

Bruck + Weckerle Architekten
www.bruck-weckerle.com
69, rue Glesener L-1631 Luxembourg
Tel: 29 71 29
E-mail: info@bruck-weckerle.com

NAOS ARCHITECTURE
www.naos.es
Plaza de Charles Darwin, 3
Perillo - Oleiros - A Coruña 15172.
Tel: 981 169 199
E-mail: arquitecturanaos@gmail.com

Croxon Ramsay
croxonramsay.com.au
25A Mollison St, Abbotsford VIC 3067
Cnr of Lt Nicholson St & Mollison St
Tel: 03 9429 1005
E-mail: mail@croxonramsay.com.au

Netzwerkarchitekten
www.netzwerkarchitekten.de
PartG. Donnersbergring 20. 64295
Darmstadt
Tel: +49 (0)6151 / 39149-0
E-mail: kontakt@netzwerkarchitekten.de

ADAM DETTRICK ARCHITECT
www.adamdettrickarchitect.com.au
305/20-22 McKillop St
Melbourne 3000, Australia
Tel: 03 9606 0774
E-mail: adam@adamdettrickarchitect.com.au

Taylor Smyth architects
www.taylorsmyth.com
245 Davenport Road, Suite 300
Toronto, Ontario, Canada M5R 1K1
Tel: 416 968 6688
E-mail: info@taylorsmyth.com

Dorte Mandrup Arkitekter ApS
www.dortemandrup.dk
Dorte Mandrup Arkitekter
Vesterbrogade 95A, 4th floor
1620 Copenhagen V, Denmark
Tel: +45 3393 7350
E-mail: info@dortemandrup.dk

Acton Ostry Architects
www.actonostry.ca
111 E 8 Avenue
Vancouver, BC V5T 1R8, Canada
Tel: 604.739.3344
E-mail: info@actonostry.ca

Mark Horton Architecture
http://www.mh-a.com
135 South Park, San Francisco, CA 94107
Tel: 415.543.3347
E-mail: info@mh-a.com

Francisco Vaz Monteiro and Filipa Roseta
www.rosetavazmonteiro.com
Rua Pinheiro Chagas nº 73, 3º Dto. 1050-176
Lisboa - Portugal
Tel: +351 213 049 375
E-mail: arquitectos@rosetavazmonteiro.com

archi5
archi5.fr
48-50 rue Voltaire
93100 Montreuil
Tel: +33 1 48 59 16 08
E-mail: contact@archi5.fr

KAW architects and advisors
www.kaw.nl
Hofstraat 8
9712 JB Groningen
postbus 1527
9701 BM Groningen
Fax: 050 - 369 58 70
E-mail: info@kaw.nl

Salto AB
www.salto.ee
Kalaranna 6, 10415 Tallinn, Estonia
Tel: +372 682 5222
E-mail: info@salto.ee

EDERER + HAGHIRIAN ARCHITEKTEN ZT-OG
http://www.keh.at
Schießstattgasse 50
A-8010 Graz, Österreich
Tel: 0316 / 682976
E-mail: office@keh.at

Pedro Quero Arquitectos, S.L.P.
Avda. Galicia, 6 - 2º Derecha
33005 Oviedo
Principado de Asturias
España
Tel: +34 985 20 50 58
E-mail: info@pedroqueroarquitectos.com

H2o architects Pty Ltd
www.h2oarchitects.com.au
29 Northumberland Street Collingwood
Victoria 3066
Australia
Tel: 61 3 9417 0900
E-mail: studio@h2oarchitects.com.au

COLBOC FRANZEN & ASSOCIES
www.cfa-arch.com
10 rue Bisson
75020 Paris
Tel: 0033(0)1 42 49 80 24
E-mail: architectes@cfa-arch.com

ACXT Architects
www.acxt.es
Plaza de las Naciones
Torre Norte, planta 9
41927 Mairena del Aljarafe.Sevilla
Tel: +34 95 560 05 28
E-mail: aroman@acxt.net

SMITH VIGEANT architectes
www.smithvigeant.com
5605 avenue de Gaspé
Bureau 601
Montréal (Québec) H2T 2A4
Tel: 514 844 7414 poste 100
E-mail: info@smithvigeant.com